AF684516

ABOUT THE LAST DAY OF JULY

How does one go from being held in a mental hospital during a psychotic episode to someone who can live on their own and then write about it? How can someone who continues to have cycles of mania and depression able to reflect back on those episodes and then write about how it felt? If you want to understand how a bipolar patient feels and their daily struggles then this is the book to read. The author made significant progress over the years but everyone should realize that there is no real "cure" for bipolar "disease". I say disease because its a chemical imbalance of the brain which we don't fully understand. Certain "triggers" can bring back some of the symptoms as the author discusses. The book also makes you wonder how bad it must be for people who don't have access to mental health professionals and if we as a country are doing enough to help these people. How many people are in jail because they didn't get help? Other more general topics/themes include giving back, helping others, living simply, and finding your purpose in life. These are things everyone should think about, not just the mentally ill. I highly recommend the book.

Tom

This is such a raw and honest book about the author's journey through mental illness. It gives a great inside to the challenges someone faces and the everyday symptoms. Even though I do not have mental illness I can relate to some battles and understand more about others. I think my favorite part is how positive his attitude continues to be through it all! Great book!!

Nyssa Darterd

This is a great account of John's life following his diagnosis in 2006 and what it's like for him to live with his bipolar one disorder every single day. He has many useful and thought-provoking insights during the course of the book, which is basically a journal he wrote on an almost daily basis. For example, on January 4, 2019, he muses: "What is my personality and what is my illness? Is it both? Was I just an active child that played sports and excelled at school or was that the beginning of mania?...When I was working 60+ hours a week and going to college full-time, was I manic or just showing a good work ethic?" These are great questions, and the reader will be surprised and pleased at some of John's answers. Highly recommend this book to anyone trying to understand their own mental illness or that of someone they care about...a nice thought collection. The only thing I think would have improved the book is if it had page numbers so it would be easier to refer back to some of John's key epiphanies.

Lori M. Balster

This is the first of Mr. Mel's books I have read. I have multiple people in my life struggling with bipolar disorder and while I see what it does on the outside, I have never had insight as to how the other person felt on the inside.

Wendi

This book is very very good. A brutally honest journal about the author's struggles with a bipolar mind and his hope for a better future. I recommend it to anyone who may be struggling with mental health issues or anyone who is willing to learn more about the effects of this disease.

Kevin C Schell

An incredibly honest and true to life story of one man's struggle to exist, A world where he is deemed insane. He struggles, he makes it through to have a promising career as a writer. Confessional, Frank, brave.

Albino Carrillo

ABOUT POEMS FROM A BIPOLAR MIND

Mr. Medl has the natural talent of being able to paint a picture with words. His poetry covers many subjects, but his imagery remains vivid and imaginative. I enjoyed the author's notes, which offered insight added context to each poem. In the end, the reader feels as if they have taken a guided journey through Medl's fascinating mind. I recommend this book on it's own or as a companion to the author's other book, "Millions Like Me". Both are great reads, and I can only hope that there will be more books to follow.

Evan Vomacka

A wonderful collection of beautifully written poems. John is clearly a poet and wonderful with prose. I've found that people with a mental illness, have absolutely wonderful minds. My mom also has bipolar, and her writing is wonderful, when she can put the discipline to sit down and do it. She's no poet, but her eulogy for grandma was absolutely heartfelt, as several other small pieces she's actually written. John's poems are clear, concise, and a promising insight into the mind of bipolar. They're beautiful, and I hope he continues to write them.

Craig A. Price Jr.

I love that John chose to add another talent to his series. Mental illness is a serious issue that often gets swept under the rug and I like that John took a different approach by embracing the disorder and providing hope and incite.

Grant Williams

Excellent poetry with excellent commentary on each poem. A look into someone's mind with mental illness with obvious creativity and talent.

Sue M

ABOUT MILLIONS LIKE ME

This man has struggled for years with his illness. He has researched it thoroughly and through personal experience he certainly understands all that he has gone through and is going through. His family must be very understanding and supportive of him. An enlightening read for me.

Ann

I. would. recommend. this. book. to. anyone. who. I. talk to. IT. was. a. very interesting. book. I enjoyed it. very much.

Robert S

A brilliant take on a man's life and struggle with mental illness. Bipolar is a condition not a lot of people understand. Even doctors are unsure about most of it. A person with bipolar is often sporadic, unrestful, and hard to concentrate. My mother has it, and so I understand it more than most. When I saw that John himself had bipolar, and wrote about his experiences, I was eager to pick up this book. I've talked to Mom over the years about it, but getting additional insight from another who had the patience to write his journey down, was inspiring. It was like hearing from a good friend. The voice for the narrative was engaging, and I consumed every word. I look forward to reading the rest of John's book for a wonderful insight into the mind of mental illness.

Craig A. Price Jr.

John has so much talent and is doing everything he can to break the stigma that mentally ill people can't function like the rest of society. Overcoming every obstacle thrown at him he has made it his mission to spread awareness of how one can recover and adapt to being productive. I enjoyed his book so much that I bought 2 copies of all five of his books. One to stock one to share.

Grant Williams

John is brave to lay bare his soul as he does in this book. It is rare that someone can look at themselves so honestly, especially someone who must admit that he is unstable and that he will always have to work to keep his mental illness under some sort of control. As he says, "Every day is a mountain." He bravely admits that he will always have mental illness but it is a part of who he is, and he is not trying to be someone he is not. Very brave...especially since talking about mental illness is still viewed as "taboo" by a significant portion of society. However, it is because of John's bravery at facing what he sees in the mirror that there is some real insight into the human condition in his prose and poetry. This book has no page numbers and many of the poems don't have names, which means while there are worthwhile insights in the book, they may be hard to refer back to once you have found them...they are more of an organic whole, a cohesive tableau of what mental illness is like. A worthwhile book. I will be reading more of John's works.

Lori M. Balster

WORKINGS OF A BIPOLAR MIND 1-3

THE INNER MIND OF SOMEONE WITH BIPOLAR DISORDER

JOHN MEDL

Formatted by Craig A. Price

CONTENTS

MILLIONS LIKE ME

POEMS FROM A BIPOLAR MIND

THE LAST DAY OF JULY

John Medl

MILLIONS
LIKE ME
MY STRUGGLE WITH MENTAL ILLNESS

INTRODUCTION

There are many purposes to this book. One is to educate and inform the reader of the disorders I have (and millions of others that are affected). Another is to help motivate and inspire those with mental illness. Lastly, I want the reader to try and see what mental illness looks like from someone who suffers from it. There are many people with no experience in these matters, and it is hard to convince some that mental illness is even an illness at all. Some people think you can will your way out of it either through diet and exercise, or positive thinking, prayer, or whatever "cure" they think there is. Some people believe mental illness affects the weak-minded. Mental illness affects people at all levels of intelligence. There are those that I could educate until I am blue in the face, but they will not be convinced otherwise. A friend described it as there being two types of people: the receptive and the non-receptive. As someone with mental illness, it's important to know the difference and focus on the ones who will be receptive. They could be receptive to a variety of things; my symptoms and feelings, for example. Just like any belief, really. Like politics or religion. I think this will end up being therapeutic for me also. I use humor a lot, even though this book isn't supposed to be humorous exactly. I may go on tangents as well. My mind skips around a lot. I am trying to paint a complete picture of what someone with mental illness goes through and where he/she may come from. Mental illness does not discriminate based on race, gender, social class, or any other personal factors. It affects everyone from all walks of life. There will be some of my poetry mixed in as well, and I will include as many poems as I have at the end of the book. I have been writing poetry since grade school, and I have continued into adulthood. 1 in 4 people are thought to have some form of mental illness. 1 in 3 go through anxiety, panic, or depression at some point in their lives. I think I have led an unusual and interesting life to this point, so the read should be enjoyable. I should probably mention that I have been diagnosed with bipolar disorder, panic disorder, and obsessive-compulsive disorder. I also have agoraphobia and claustrophobia.

1 SYMPTOMS OF BIPOLAR DISORDER

MANIC PHASE OF BIPOLAR DISORDER

SIGNS AND SYMPTOMS OF THE MANIC OR HYPOMANIC PHASE OF BIPOLAR disorder can include:

- Euphoria
- Inflated self-esteem
- Poor judgment
- Rapid speech
- Racing thoughts
- Aggressive behavior
- Agitation or irritation
- Increased physical activity
- Risky behavior
- Spending sprees or unwise financial choices
- Increased drive to perform or achieve goals
- Increased sex drive
- Decreased need for sleep
- Easily distracted
- Careless or dangerous use of drugs or alcohol

- Frequent absences from work or school
- Delusions or a break from reality (psychosis)
- Poor performance at work or school

DEPRESSIVE PHASE OF BIPOLAR DISORDER

Signs and symptoms of the depressive phase of bipolar disorder can include:

- Sadness
- Hopelessness
- Suicidal thoughts or behavior
- Anxiety
- Guilt
- Sleep problems
- Low appetite or increased appetite
- Fatigue
- Loss of interest in activities once considered enjoyable
- Problems concentrating
- Irritability
- Chronic pain without a known cause
- Frequent absences from work or school
- Poor performance at work or school

OTHER SIGNS AND SYMPTOMS OF BIPOLAR DISORDER

Signs and symptoms of bipolar disorder can also include:

- Seasonal changes in mood. As with seasonal affective disorder (SAD), some people with bipolar disorder have moods that change with the seasons. Some people become manic or hypomanic in the spring or summer and then become depressed in the fall or winter. For other people, this cycle is reversed — they become depressed in the spring or summer and manic or hypomanic in the fall or winter.
- Rapid cycling bipolar disorder. Some people with bipolar disorder have rapid mood shifts. This is defined as having four or more mood

swings within a single year. However, in some people, mood shifts occur much more quickly, sometimes within just hours.

- Psychosis. Severe episodes of either mania or depression may result in psychosis, a detachment from reality. Symptoms of psychosis may include false but strongly held beliefs (delusions) and hearing or seeing things that aren't there (hallucinations). Courtesy of mayoclinic.com

2 WHAT ARE PANIC ATTACKS/PANIC DISORDER?

A discrete period of intense fear or discomfort, in which four (or more) of the following symptoms developed abruptly and reached a peak within 10 minutes:

1. palpitations, pounding heart, or accelerated heart rate
2. sweating
3. trembling or shaking
4. sensations of shortness of breath or smothering
5. feeling of choking
6. chest pain or discomfort
7. nausea or abdominal distress
8. feeling dizzy, unsteady, lightheaded, or faint
9. derealization (feelings of unreality) or depersonalization (being detached from oneself)
10. fear of losing control or going crazy
11. fear of dying
12. paresthesias (numbness or tingling sensations)
13. chills or hot flushes

DSM IV Criteria for Panic Disorder

A) Both (1) and (2)

(1) recurrent unexpected Panic Attacks

(2) at least one of the attacks has been followed by 1 month (or more) of one (or more) of the following:

(a) persistent concern about having additional attacks

(b) worry about the implications of the attack or its consequences (e.g., losing control, having a heart attack, "going crazy")

(c) a significant change in behavior related to the attacks

B) The Panic Attacks are not due to the direct physiological effects of a substance (e.g., a drug of abuse, a medication) or a general medical condition (e.g., hyperthyroidism).

C) The Panic Attacks are not better accounted for by another mental disorder, such as Social Phobia (e.g., occurring on exposure to feared social situations), Specific Phobia (e.g., on exposure to a specific phobic situation), Obsessive-Compulsive Disorder (e.g., on exposure to dirt in someone with an obsession about contamination),

Posttraumatic Stress Disorder (e.g., in response to stimuli associated with a severe stressor), or Separation Anxiety Disorder (e.g., in response to being away from home or close relatives).

Panic Disorder is divided into with or without agoraphobia DSM IV Criteria for Agoraphobia

A) anxiety about being in places or situations from which escape might be difficult (or embarrassing) or in which help may not be available in the event of having an unexpected or situationally predisposed Panic Attack or panic-like symptoms. Agoraphobic fears typically involve characteristic clusters of situations that include being outside the home alone; being in a crowd, or standing in a line; being on a bridge; and traveling in a bus, train, or automobile.

B) The situations are avoided (e.g., travel is restricted) or else are endured with marked distress or with anxiety about having a Panic Attack or panic-like symptoms, or require the presence of a companion.

C) The anxiety or phobic avoidance is not better accounted for by another mental disorder, such as Social Phobia (e.g., avoidance limited to social situations because of fear of embarrassment), Specific Phobia (e.g., avoidance limited to a single situation like elevators), Obsessive-Compulsive Disorder (e.g., avoidance of dirt in someone with an obsession about contamination), Posttraumatic Stress Disorder (e.g., avoidance of stimuli associated with a severe stressor), or Separation Anxiety Disorder (e.g., avoidance of leaving home or relatives).

3 OBSESSIVE-COMPULSIVE DISORDER SYMPTOMS INCLUDE BOTH OBSESSIONS AND COMPULSIONS

Obsession symptoms

OCD obsessions are repeated, persistent and unwanted ideas, thoughts, images or impulses that you have involuntarily and that seem to make no sense. These obsessions typically intrude when you're trying to think of or do other things.

Obsessions often have themes to them, such as:

- Fear of contamination or dirt
- Having things orderly and symmetrical
- Aggressive or horrific impulses
- Sexual images or thoughts

Obsession symptoms and signs may include:

- Fear of being contaminated by shaking hands or by touching objects others have touched
- Doubts that you've locked the door or turned off the stove
- Thoughts that you've hurt someone in a traffic accident
- Intense stress when objects aren't orderly or facing the right way
- Images of hurting your child

- Impulses to shout obscenities in inappropriate situations
- Avoidance of situations that can trigger obsessions, such as shaking hands
- Replaying pornographic images in your mind
- Dermatitis because of frequent hand washing
- Skin lesions because of picking at your skin
- Hair loss or bald spots because of hair pulling

Compulsion symptoms

OCD compulsions are repetitive behaviors that you feel driven to perform. These repetitive behaviors are meant to prevent or reduce anxiety related to your obsessions. For instance, if you believe you hit someone with your car, you may return to the apparent scene over and over because you just can't shake your doubts. You may also make up rules or rituals to follow that help control the anxiety you feel when having obsessive thoughts.

As with obsessions, compulsions typically have themes, such as:

- Washing and cleaning
- Counting
- Checking
- Demanding reassurances
- Performing the same action repeatedly
- Orderliness

Compulsion symptoms and signs may include:

- Hand washing until your skin becomes raw
- Checking doors repeatedly to make sure they're locked
- Checking the stove repeatedly to make sure it's off
- Counting in certain patterns
- Arranging your canned goods to face the same way

Symptoms usually begin gradually and tend to vary in severity throughout your life. Symptoms generally worsen during times when you're experiencing more stress. OCD is considered a lifelong illness.

When to see a doctor

There's a difference between being a perfectionist and having obsessive-compulsive disorder. Perhaps you keep the floors in your house so clean that you could eat off them. Or you like your knickknacks arranged just so. That doesn't necessarily mean that you have obsessive-compulsive disorder.

Obsessive-compulsive disorder can be so severe and time-consuming that it literally becomes disabling. You may be able to do little else but spend time on your obsessions and compulsions — washing your hands for hours each day, for instance. With OCD, you may have a low quality of life because the condition rules most of your days. You may be very distressed, but you seem powerless to stop your urges. Most adults can recognize that their obsessions and compulsions don't make sense. Children, however, may not understand what's wrong.

If your obsessions and compulsions are affecting your life, see your doctor or mental health provider. People with OCD may be ashamed and embarrassed about the condition. But even if your rituals are deeply ingrained, treatment can help.

4 DSM IV PSYCHIATRIC DISORDERS

THE DSM IV IS A MANUAL USED TO CHARACTERIZE VARIOUS PSYCHIATRIC disorders. Here's how it is organized:

The DSM-IV organizes each psychiatric diagnosis into five levels (axes) relating to different aspects of disorder or disability:

- Axis I: clinical disorders, including major mental disorders, as well as developmental and learning disorders
- Axis II: underlying pervasive or personality conditions, as well as mental retardation
- Axis III: Acute medical conditions and physical disorders.
- Axis IV: psychosocial and environmental factors contributing to the disorder
- Axis V: Global Assessment of Functioning or Children's Global Assessment Scale for children and teens under the age of 18. (on a scale from 100 to 1)

Common Axis I disorders include depression, anxiety disorders, bipolar disorder, ADHD, phobias, and schizophrenia.Common Axis II disorders include personality disorders: paranoid personality disorder, schizoid personality disorder, schizotypal personality disorder, borderline personality disorder, antisocial personality disorder, narcissistic personality disorder, histrionic personality disorder, avoidant personality disorder, dependent personality disorder, obsessive-compulsive personality disorder, and mental retardation.

Common Axis III disorders include brain injuries and other medical/physical disorders which may aggravate existing diseases or present symptoms similar to other disorders.

http://uk.answers.yahoo.com/question/index?qid=20090401065653AAaGyf3

5 MY BIPOLAR DISORDER

The type of bipolar disorder I have is called bipolar I with psychotic tendencies or episodes. This means that I am more manic than depressed, whereas bipolar II is vice versa. The psychotic features part, or tendencies, refers to bouts of psychosis mixed in.

A group of illnesses which disrupt the functioning of the brain which causes a condition called psychosis. Psychosis is a syndrome seen in a number of different illnesses including Schizophrenia, Schizoaffective Disorder, Delusional Disorder, Brief Psychotic Disorder, Bipolar Disorder, Major Depression or occurring as a result of the effects of illicit substances or some physical illnesses.

It consists of such symptoms as:

- Delusions - which are false beliefs that are utterly true to the one who is experiencing the psychosis, but not understandable to others from the same cultural background.
- Hallucinations - which are sensory experiences which seem entirely real to the person experiencing them, but are unable to be shared by others (e.g. hearing "voices").
- Disorganised thought, speech, or behaviour.

These symptoms may lead to social withdrawal and reduced performance in academic or occupational pursuits. The person's behaviour may change significantly. These changes may be difficult for others to understand because they occur in response to the delusions or hallucinations.

Most people are able to recover from an episode of psychosis. http://www.health.qld.gov.au/mentalhealth/abt_mental/facts_psychosis.asp

There are so many negatives that go along with this disorder, but I would not have had the energy to work and attend college and eventually graduate without these manic episodes. I try to see the positives that have come from this diagnosis. I was definitely caught up in the pursuit of financial success, and when I was diagnosed and the years after, I began to appreciate the smaller things in life. Like just living outside of the hospital. Like being able to think somewhat clearly without being delusional or psychotic. Like having food, clothing, and shelter. The one thing I miss is that I cannot read anymore. Not that I am illiterate, but my concentration and attention have deteriorated to the point of near nonexistence. That's why I am proud of this piece of work. I am passionate about helping others and sharing my story. I guess some things can hold my attention if I have enough passion about the purpose. Even TV shows are hard for me to follow. I think TV is really the lowest form of attention you can have, and it is hard for me. I watch a lot of sports, which I can kind of tune in and out of. I am pretty good with sports history though, like who is the all-time leader in whichever statistical category.

6 PANIC DISORDER

Panic disorder is my secondary diagnosis. I was diagnosed around 2009. This diagnosis is just as terrible as bipolar disorder. The physical sensations during a panic disorder are far from pleasant, and I have thought I was going to die on several occasions. I have had to go to the hospital as a result. Sometimes, even when I know it is a panic attack, it feels so real that I think I need medical attention. My last hospital visit I was there for 4 hours, and they didn't really do anything for me except give me oxygen. They listed the reason for admission as mania and panic. I have listed the symptoms previously in the book, so refer to them if you need to.

7 OBSESSIONAL OCD

THERE ARE FIVE TYPES OF OCD, AND MY TYPE IS CALLED AN OBSESSIONAL. MOST people think that people with OCD are all neat freaks, but that's not me. I don't need things in a certain order, but I don't like change. I guess I have my own order of things that may not look organized to anyone else. I hate when my mom moves things around in her attempts to clean up or organize things the way she wants. In my unprofessional opinion, she has OCD also. I should mention I live with both of my parents, who are both in their seventies. I tend to recite prayers and song lyrics in my head obsessively, as well as facts and figures. I obsessively check the clock around my med times, which are not set in stone, but for some reason, I have made it that way. I also obsessively check my eBay sales, Facebook, and/or emails. I have nervous tics like pulling at my shirt or hat, and it's hard for me to sit still sometimes. I also smoke cigarettes, which could be obsessional, or I might like the oral fixation or, on the simplest level, addicted to nicotine. Or all of the above, which is usually the answer in psychology. A disproportionate amount of the mentally ill are smokers compared with the general population. I can't smoke in my parents' house where I live now, so I am always out on the front porch.

My parents have lived in this house where I live now since 1967, and many people in my neighborhood know me and my family. I enjoy when people wave to me when they are traveling to or from work or just out and about. I like the small-town feel, and I couldn't imagine living in a big city. I would much rather live in the middle of nowhere, although there are scary parts about that to me as well. My parents' house is the only place I have ever felt like was my home. Maybe one day it will be mine. I would be proud to carry on the legacy of the household my siblings and I grew up in.

8 CLAUSTROPHOBIA

Claustrophobia is an anxiety disorder; the sufferer has an irrational fear of having no escape or being closed in. It frequently results in panic attack and can be triggered by certain stimuli or situations, such as being in a crowded elevator, a room without windows, or sitting in an airplane. Some people may even experience claustrophobia when wearing tight-necked clothing.

The word claustrophobia originates from Latin claustrum which means "a shut in place" and Greek phobos, which means "fear". Research has shown that approximately 6% of people suffer the disorder worldwide, but the majority are not receiving treatment for it.

People with claustrophobia can find the disorder hard to live with, as they will go to great lengths to avoid small spaces and situations that trigger their panic and anxiety. They will avoid certain places like the subway/underground and will prefer to take the stairs over using a lift/elevator, no matter how many floors they need to ascend/descend.

According to Medilexicon's medical dictionary, claustrophobia is: "A morbid fear of being in a confined place."

WHAT ARE THE SYMPTOMS OF CLAUSTROPHOBIA?

A symptom is something the patient feels or reports, while a sign is something that other people, including the doctor detects. A headache may be an example of a symptom, while a rash may be an example of a sign.

A claustrophobic may suffer symptoms similar to anxiety that are triggered by being in a small space. The phobia of the small space is based on the fear of running out of oxygen, along with the fear of restriction. When in an small confined space, someone with claustrophobia may start to show the following symptoms:

- Sweating
- Accelerated heart rate
- Increased blood pressure
- Hyperventilation, or 'over-breathing'
- Shaking
- Sweating
- Panic attacks
- Light-headedness
- Nausea
- Fainting
- Fear of actual harm or illness

It is not essentially the small spaces that trigger the anxiety but the fear of what can happen to the person if confined to that area, hence the fear of running out of oxygen. Examples of small spaces that could trigger a claustrophobic's anxiety are:

- elevators/lifts
- basements/cellars
- small rooms
- airplanes
- locked rooms
- cars
- trains
- crowded areas

As claustrophobia is also defined by the phobia of being restricted, being confined to one area can also trigger the anxiety (e.g. having to wait in line at a checkout/cash register). There have also been studies to support the theory that MRI machines can cause claustrophobia due to the prolonged length of time spent in a confined space with restricted movement.

As the above situations can cause a claustrophobic to suffer anxiety and panic attacks, a claustrophobic will try their best to avoid them. The following are examples of how a claustrophobic may behave:

- As soon as they enter a room, they may urgently check out where the exits are and position themselves near them. When all the doors are closed, they may feel troubled.
- In a crowded party, even if the venue is a large and spacious room, they will position themselves near the door.
- Avoid driving during peak times, when traffic is likely to be congested
- Avoid travelling as a passenger in a car during peak traffic times
- In severe cases, some individuals with claustrophobia may panic when a door is closed
- Avoid using elevators and use the stairs, even if this means getting tired, out of breath and sweating a lot

WHAT CAUSES CLAUSTROPHOBIA?

Claustrophobia is generally the result of an experience in the person's past (usually in their childhood) that has led them to associate small spaces with the feeling of panic or being in imminent danger. Examples of these kinds of past experiences are:

- falling into a deep pool and not being able to swim
- being in a crowded area and getting separated from parents/group
- crawling into a hole and getting lost/stuck

As the experience will have dealt some kind of trauma to the person, it will affect their ability to deal with a similar situation rationally. The mind links the small space/confined area to the feeling of being in danger and the body then reacts accordingly (or how it thinks it should). This type of cause is known as classic conditioning and can also be a behavior inherited from parents or peers. If for example, a claustrophobic has a child, the child may observe their parent's behavior and develop the same fears.

There are other theories behind the causes of claustrophobia, these are:

- Smaller Amygdala - the amygdala is a tiny part of the brain that is used to control how the body processes fear. During a study, Fumi Hayano discovered that people who suffered panic disorders had a smaller amygdale than average. This smaller size could interfere with how the body processes panic and anxiety.
- Prepared Phobia - there is also a theory that phobias develop on the genetic level rather than psychologically. The research behind this theory suggests that claustrophobia and some other phobias are dormant evolutionary survival mechanisms. A survival instinct buried within our genetic code that was once crucial to human survival but is no longer needed.

HOW IS CLAUSTROPHOBIA DIAGNOSED?

Claustrophobia would be diagnosed as a result of seeing a psychologist. The patient may be seeing the psychologist because they suffer the symptoms of claustrophobia, or they could be originally seeing them about another anxiety problem or phobia.

The psychologist would ask for a description of the symptoms and what triggers them. Using their knowledge and resources, the psychologist would then determine the type and severity of the patient's phobia.

There are methods put in place to help decide if the patient is suffering from claustrophobia and to what extent. These methods are:

- Claustrophobia questionnaire - Originally developed in 1993 and modified in 2001, this has been a helpful way of identifying the symptoms of claustrophobia.
- Claustrophobia Scale - Developed in 1979, this method is made up of 20 questions that when answered can help establish the levels of anxiety when diagnosing the claustrophobia.

HOW IS CLAUSTROPHOBIA TREATED?

After diagnosis has been made, the psychologist would try one or a few of the following methods to help the claustrophobic deal with their fear:

- CBT (Cognitive-Behavioral Therapy) - This is a well-recognized treatment method for many other types of anxiety disorder. The goal of CBT is to retrain the claustrophobic's brain to no longer feel threatened by the places they fear. An approach taken may be slowly exposing the patient to small spaces and helping them deal with their fear and anxiety (in vivo exposure). This is the most common way claustrophobia is treated.
- Drug Therapy - This type of therapy can help manage the anxiety symptoms, however it does not deal with the problem itself. This, along with the undesired side effects makes this method far from first choice for treating claustrophobia.
- Relaxation Exercises - Taking deep breaths, meditating and doing muscle relaxing exercises are effective at dealing with negative thoughts and anxiety.
- Alternative/Natural medicine - There are some natural products and homeopathic medicines that some patients say help them manage panic and anxiety.

Written by Mike Paddock
Original article date: 3 Feb 2006 Article updated: 22 April 2011

9 MEDICATION

I AM ON SEVERAL MEDICATIONS TO HELP WITH MY SYMPTOMS, BUT AS YOU WILL read, do not always do the job. Presently, I am on three mood stabilizers and two anti-anxiety medications. Specifically, Invega, Trileptal, Cogentin, Klonopin, and Xanax.

1. Invega (paliperidone) is an antipsychotic medication. It works by changing the effects of chemicals in the brain.
2. Invega is used to treat schizophrenia.
3. Invega may also be used for purposes not listed in this medication guide.
4. Trileptal (oxcarbazepine) is in a group of drugs called anticonvulsants, or antiepileptic drugs. It works by decreasing nerve impulses that cause seizures.
5. Trileptal is used to treat partial seizures in adults and children who are at least 2 years old. Trileptal may also be used for purposes not listed in this medication guide.
6. Cogentin/Benztropine reduces the effects of certain chemicals in the body that may become unbalanced as a result of disease (such as Parkinson's), drug therapy, or other causes.

7. Benztropine is used to treat the symptoms of Parkinson's disease, such as muscle spasms, stiffness, tremors, sweating, drooling, and poor muscle control.
8. Benztropine is also used to treat and prevent these symptoms when they are caused by drugs such as chlorpromazine (Thorazine), fluphenazine (Prolixin), perphenazine (Trilafon), and others.
9. Benztropine may also be used for purposes not listed in this medication guide.
10. Klonopin (clonazepam) is in a group of drugs called benzodiazepines (ben-zoe-dye-AZE-eh-peens). Clonazepam affects chemicals in the brain that may become unbalanced and cause anxiety.
11. Klonopin is used to treat seizure disorders or panic disorder.
12. Klonopin may also be used for purposes not listed in this medication guide.
13. Xanax (alprazolam) belongs to a group of drugs called benzodiazepines. It works by slowing down the movement of chemicals in the brain that may become unbalanced. This results in a reduction in nervous tension (anxiety).
14. Xanax is used to treat anxiety disorders, panic disorders, and anxiety caused by depression. Xanax may also be used for purposes not listed in this medication guide.

1-5 drug information found at www.drugs.com if you want to read more about side effects or other uses.

Medication regimens tend to be switched when necessary, either the drug itself or a different dosage. I have gone years without changing a thing, but just recently had to change in June 2012, but I will explain that later. The biggest side effect of my medications is lethargy. I sleep most of the day, and my days and nights are reversed. Most times, I wake up at 2AM, ready to start the day.

10 A WORK OF TRUTH

THIS BOOK IS NOT FICTIONAL WHATSOEVER, BUT IT MAY BE LIKE A STORY. THE POINT of some of my stories is to show how stress may have triggered a breakdown, and also to show how out of control I was. It's a very odd feeling to look back at my past and realize how foolish I acted, when, in those moments, I didn't realize it. I also tend to be too hard on myself. I can't help that I was being manic. When you are in a manic episode, you feel terrific and just keep going and going with energy to no end. When the mania is over, sometimes the events that happened when you were in mania or psychosis are hard to remember. I just remembered I had a great time. Part of my erratic behavior could also come from my fear of being forgotten. I wanted to live my life, so that whoever meets me or is friends with me, will remember me. If you are not remembered when you are gone, it's like you never existed, in my opinion. I think I have already accomplished that. On the flip side, I believe if you are remembered, it's like you are never gone.

People with bipolar disorder can sometimes be the "life of the party", and that role seemed to fit me rather well. I like being a little wild and out of control. I like stirring things up, and making lasting memories as a result of that wildness, or whatever you want to call it. The way I see it, there are two types of people; the people who ask why, and the people who say why not. I am a why not kind of person. I have settled down quite a lot, and I don't go out much. Most of the time, I am happy staying home and sober. Every once in a while, I get a little manic and want to drink and party with my friends.

I would describe myself today as a social binge drinker. I don't drink alone, but I did in college after work to wind down for the day. I think I am really a social drinker at heart. When I am around my friends, I just want to get wild, and I usually drink to excess. I used to drink to the point of getting sick, but that was more in my younger days. I still did get sick on occasion in my late twenties. I never really feel any peer pressure, it's just that drinking to me is normalcy. It's what I'm used to. I feel restricted if I can't do things I used to do. The fact is that people change, regardless of mental state. It's just hard to accept that I may be turning the page and slowing down.

Some of the events may be out of chronological order because my memory is so bad. I will do the best I can, and I may have to refer to my medical records to be accurate, which, by the way, is as thick as a dictionary. Somehow, I keep getting denied Social Security Disability. In my most recent rejection letter, the SSA (Social Security Administration) will not even grant me the time of day to appeal the denial. Sometimes I may set things from my medical records aside with quotation marks, other times, I will be reciting from memory. Maybe a little game the reader could play is taking the aforementioned symptoms and apply them to my life and the stories I will tell. If you want to play psychologist. If not, enjoy the read.

With all that out of the way, I guess I will just start at the beginning, and let it flow. I was born in 1981 in a suburb of Cincinnati, Ohio, to my 39-year-old mother and my 40-year-old father. I was a "pleasant surprise" as they like to say. I always tease I was an accident. It doesn't matter how I got here because I am here now. I have four older siblings, three brothers and a sister, ranging in age from 48 to 41. I am now 31 years old. My siblings used to always tease me that I was adopted, and I think I believed it sometimes until about age eight. I think I finally demanded I be shown my birth certificate. My parents got married in 1963 and are still married to this day. They are coming up on 50 years of marriage. My neighborhood has basically a small-town feel. Everyone knows each other kind of thing. Middle class at best. I never went without the necessities and had few expensive things like other kids I knew. I didn't mind too much. It made me appreciate what I had; which was a solid family, and I was completely immersed in sports. Those are the great memories I have from my childhood.

I actually had a life-changing moment at the age of 5 (maybe younger), which I remember to this day. I was born with a giant nevus (basically a mole) that covered my entire leg when I was born. The nevus could have potentially become cancerous later in life, so doctors had to remove it and do a skin graft to replace the skin. I was in a cast for about six months, around the age of two. This left a lot of scar tissue, and the color of my left leg is a darker than my right. My left leg is skinnier than my right also. One day, I was playing with friends, and some kid called me "bacon leg". I was devastated. I sat on my porch and cried for at least an hour. That was the first time in my life I realized I looked different and was being made fun of for it. When I was done crying, I had an epiphany of sorts and decided that I would never treat someone like that kid did to me that day. It felt awful, and I never wanted to make anyone feel that way. It's funny that I still remember that.

I had a good childhood, in general. My father was the breadwinner and authoritarian, and my mother raised the children and kept house. Very old-fashioned and traditional. My father was not very emotional, and my mother was somewhat over emotional. I think I have only seen my dad cry once or twice, and telling me he loves me with the same frequency. That is how it was. You were just supposed to know, even if you really needed to hear it sometimes. My mother still had a traditional job when times were economically tough. In her seventies now, she still works. My mother did everything around the house. She always had dinner on the table when my father got off work, and she considered it a time for everyone in the family to catch up on what had happened that day. She still cooks dinner almost every night for my dad, except for the rare occasions they go out to dinner. My mom and my sister were basically the ones to raise me, teach me, and so forth. One of my brothers also helped. He used to tote me around and show me off to all his friends. My dad's job was to work, take care of the yard, or any other "manly" things like fixing things. He probably missed 5 days of work in 50 years, if that. He was very hardworking, and I always admired him for that. He had a bit of a temper, and would take it out on the kids sometimes physically, but I don't think he missed more than a handful of my baseball games. My parents were never drinkers, and physical violence was rare, but present. Being older now, I realize my father doesn't know how to express his emotions or communicate very well, so anger, violence, bitterness, and sarcasm was how it came out. He still doesn't know how to communicate, which doesn't surprise me. I don't think it is realistic to think he would all of a sudden change. I also played soccer, basketball, and lacrosse, to which games he rarely attended. He didn't go either because he didn't like these sports or he was just too tired from working. Either way, it would have been nice for him to be there. I tried baseball, football, and track and field in high school, but I wasn't as talented as the other kids. Maybe I wasn't as dedicated, either. I had mixed feelings towards my father, and I still do to this day.

I started reading before the age of 2, and I think people started to notice then that I was a pretty bright child. I was very social and enjoyed talking to people older than myself. I don't know if it was because I associated more with older people because my parents are older or what, or if I was socially mature for my age, maybe because of my older siblings. I was raised Catholic, and attended Mass every Sunday until about the age of 15. I refused to go one Sunday because I felt like everyone was going through the motions and forgot everything they were supposed to learn as soon as Mass let out. I didn't think that was right. I wasn't sure of my own faith either, so I didn't think it was right for me to go for that reason either. My parents were big believers in private Catholic schooling, so I can only imagine the outrageous amounts of money it cost to send all five children through private grade school and high school. I have to give them credit for being so unselfish because they could have had a lot more money freed up if we all had been sent to public school.

I found school very boring, but managed to make As or Bs all the way through college for the most part. I also worked the entire time to try to support myself the best I could in high school and college. I held a full-time job while attending college full time. My parents were always there to help me financially if I couldn't make the bills. At the worst financial times, I didn't know where my next meal was going to come from, and once, I had to sleep in my apartment with no electricity for 3 days. I regularly got in trouble for talking too much or clowning around in grade school and high school. I earned a B.A. In Psychology from the University of Dayton. I even had conflicts with some of my professors over attendance policies and what I thought was unfair subjective grading. Once again, this could have been a result of my bipolar disorder building up and having problems with authority. Or my points were valid, or both. Later, I would earn a real estate license. I had grand plans of being a millionaire, real estate mogul.

My entrance test scores for high school were nearly perfect, and I attended high school where my three brothers had gone also. I held various jobs since the age of 15, mostly of the pizza or food delivery variety. I played nearly every sport when I was a child, but could not compete with the athletes at my high school, so that is when my sports career ended. I wasn't used to being average, or even below, I guess. I don't really enjoy playing games I don't have a chance at winning. I can be a sore winner, all in fun, but I would like to think of myself as a gracious loser. I was always big and tall and towered over most children. Not the case in high school. I went to Archbishop Moeller High School, which is nationally recognized for academic and athletic excellence. I was 3rd in my class academically and after freshmen year, and would finish 22giving. I had a photographic memory in my schooling days, and I rarely studied. Maybe I just retained everything the first time. I was skipping high school and smoking a lot of marijuana. A lot of those days were spent bumming around, usually at a park just listening to new music or throwing a frisbee. Eventually, my friends and I got caught after we left fake voice messages on the school voice mail, pretending to be each other's parents. I think it was the bursting out laughing that gave us away. We were reprimanded, and we never missed a day after that. I got into photography as well. Taking pictures of nature was my interest, and I still enjoy that to this day. I went to the many parks in Cincinnati, and I took pictures of simple things like a flower arrangement or a fountain, which is amazing considering the lack of effort I was.

There was a place a lot of my friends went to hang out in high school that we called "the band room". It was my friend's upper loft in his garage where he kept his drums. He went to a public school in the area, but I had known him from sports as a child. We had lots of good times there, and his parents tolerated us as long as we didn't get too out of control. It was a place we could all go to hang out without much parental supervision. We would drink, smoke pot, and do other drugs occasionally up there. I had three girls as my best friends in high school, and two of them I went to grade school with for eight years. We used to drive around and listen to music and smoke pot, sometimes through a rich neighborhood in Cincinnati. We hung out all the time. One time we were smoking pot, and I thought I saw my deceased grandmother's face up in the clouds. It really frightened me at first, and then comforted me like she was still with me in spirit. I realize now I could have just been high, or it was a precursor hallucination from bipolar disorder.

I got along with the jocks, hippies, nerds, and everyone else. I was very outgoing and likeable. My high school was an all male high school, so ribbing and making fun of each other was a daily thing.

If you couldn't take it, you wouldn't survive. The best defense was to give it right back, and I did. I was basically a smartass, and have been my whole life. The students took a liking to that. The authority figures that didn't appreciate my humor reprimanded me for it. Some teachers actually knew how to handle me, to their credit, and would tolerate me to a certain point. I knew when to quit with these teachers because I respected them for putting up with me and teaching me so much. Not just the subject they taught, but a little about adult life along the way. The whole dynamic of my high school was to prepare you for college and manhood, and it did. I shrugged it off like it didn't, just to not give satisfaction to the higher-ups that saw me as a nuisance. There was a prayer retreat that was optional for seniors, and I was one of the two who did not attend out of a class of over 200. They acted like it was optional, but all the authority figures were not pleased I didn't go.

I earned a partial academic scholarship to the University of Dayton on account of my high ACT score, which was really a drop in the bucket considering how expensive it was. My SAT scores were in the 1100s, which really isn't that great, considering how smart I thought I was. I was lucky to score better on the ACT, with a score of 29. I guess that is good enough to get a partial scholarship. They called the University of Dayton "Moeller North" because so many people from my Cincinnati high school go there. I still have student loans to pay back from attending. I learned there is a program for the disabled to have student loan debt relieved, if deemed by the doctor and the courts. That is what I am pursuing now. I have been living my mental illness for 7 years, and the state and federal courts refuse to grant me disability. I don't think I ever will pay those student loans back, honestly. It's the only debt I have. All my credit cards got paid off with help from my father, and I am very grateful for that. He even helped with some of my student loans. I would gradually pay him back most of it.

I never met my maternal grandfather or my paternal grandmother. They both passed before I was born. I've never heard too many stories about my paternal grandmother, just that she was a farmer and a very nice lady. My grandfather would end up remarrying (too soon, according to his kids AKA my dad, aunt, and uncle). His second wife was the only grandmother I would know on my dad's side. She was very good with money, and passed away, leaving my grandfather a widower for the second time. She was a big believer in education and was always a very sweet lady to me. My grandfather passed away in 2012. He fought in WWII in the United States Navy aboard the USS Whitley. He was a mechanic for the ship. He could fix or build pretty much anything. We have an American flag in a case in our dining room commemorating his service. I never saw such a flag in real life before. I always saw them handed to families at funerals on TV or in the movies. Soon after he died, it gave me a creepy feeling, but now, it makes me proud I am his grandson. We also got a letter from President Obama thanking our family for his service. Another proud moment.

From the stories my mom tells, my maternal grandfather would have loved me. He was a drinker, smoker, gambler, and an accomplished businessman. He was also honored as a Kentucky State Colonel. He used to feed the homeless and poor right out of his own home, with my grandmother (my mom's mom). I feel like things started to go downhill when my maternal grandmother passed in 1998. I was 16 or 17 years old. The night she died, I went into my room with a fifth of whiskey and closed the door. Probably the first time I was really drunk. I remember crying too. I was no longer in sports activities. I began drinking and smoking marijuana. I experimented with mushrooms and ecstasy also. I tried acid and smoked hash oil once, and smoked opium whenever it was available, which was hardly ever. Mostly at music festivals and rock concerts. I never snorted anything in my life, nor did I ever shoot heroin or anything like that. I ate a piece of cocaine once because one of my friends always had it, but like I said, never snorted it. I quit all the drugs by age 20, except for smoking pot. The reason I quit the harder drugs is because I took too many psychedelic mushrooms and had a bad trip, as they call it. Wild, intense hallucinations, and that was the end of that. The walls and floor were moving and vibrating. I passed out in my kitchen in my apartment and woke up terrified and confused. A part of me is glad I experimented, but I don't think I could encourage any child to try what I did in good conscience. I continued to smoke marijuana every day, several times a day. It never really cost me a lot of money, because I was selling it to my friends, or at least, people who I thought were my friends.

Everyone is your friend when you have something they want. I started out small, just straight out buying it. Then, I met a few people who had more, at a discounted rate. I began to realize if I sold it; I didn't have to pay for it.

That's how I got into the whole drug dealing situation. I don't like the term "drug dealer" because of the stereotype that goes with it. I didn't hurt anyone, and I wasn't on the street selling it to kids. I didn't own any guns either. I really just sold it to my friends, and I have a lot. Sometimes I would have to ride to bad parts of town to get it cheaper, which was pretty risky now that I look back on it. The guy who would take me to these neighborhoods always had a gun strapped to him under his armpit. He never had to use it when I was around, but it made me feel safer. I met him through a mutual friend, and we even hung out sometimes despite the fifteen years or so age difference. He was my first supplier. In college, I immediately found a supplier. It was all I knew how to get it for cheap and smoke for free. If I was lucky, I would even make money. Actually, I made 100% on my money, but I smoked a lot, which cut into the profits significantly. I got into it pretty heavy, transporting somewhat large amounts from Dayton to Cincinnati and back. I think I liked the easy money, the power, and the respect I got from my "customers". People tend to kiss your ass when you are supplying them. I even got respect from my dealers because I made them all so much money. Never mind that some days I could have easily gone to prison if I had been caught. I had nerves of steel. I don't know why I didn't really care. It could have been the money, or maybe I felt important. I was young too, and sometimes you feel invincible. I hope you are following my skipping around from ideas to memories. You may be asking yourself: Where were his parents at? They were both working most of the time, and I really quit listening to them when I got my first car at the age of 16. I had a job, my own money, and my own transportation. I got away with pretty much anything. I would disappear for the whole weekend while I was not in school. My mom still thinks she failed me, and she could have done more. I tell her all the time she was a good mom, and I wouldn't have listened, anyway. The most despicable behavior I displayed when I was young was stealing money and pain medication from her. It was never much, but I regret it so much. I hate thieves, and I used to be one of them.

When I was a child, my father used to say I had a "spring in my ass" because I would never sit still. That could have been a clue that I would turn out to have bipolar disorder, but a lot of kids were hyper, like I was. It may sound funny, but my obsession with numbers began with the Count from Sesame Street. I remember I used to spend days writing out numbers, starting at one and continuing into the tens of thousands. Pretty strange for someone not quite five years old.

When I was a teenager, I started going to music festivals and rock concerts. I loved it. I felt like the people understood me there and thought like me to some extent. I enjoyed traveling to them as well, from Florida to Vermont. It really changed me. I didn't realize that there were so many people that "went against the grain" of societal norms and mores. The people dressed and acted much differently than the people I encountered in parochial school. I started with a music festival called Hookahville, which was named because the head-lining band was called Ekoostik Hookah. There were a lot of other bands, too. I got to see Blues Traveler, Arlo Guthrie, Ziggy Marley, and many other great bands. It was a three-day event every Memorial Day and Labor Day weekends. I probably attended around seven of those. I went to a Phish concert in Florida on a Seminole Indian reservation that had over 110,000 people. One of the best times of my life. Phish is a jam band with a cult following similar to the Grateful Dead. I was 18, and it was New Year's Eve 2000. It was a three-day event. It was an awesome and eye-opening experience. People were walking around naked, doing drugs, basically total freedom. Police were not allowed on the reservation because it is considered out of the jurisdiction of the state or federal government. Two people died that weekend. While it is a tragedy, all things considered, could have been worse. They even showed part of the concert on the Dick Clark's New Year's Eve countdown show. Phish is the name of the band I have seen most, and the atmosphere of those shows stayed with me. I still try to go whenever I can. It's hard for me to handle large crowds. It's hit or miss. Sometimes it bothers me, sometimes it doesn't, but is severe enough to label me agoraphobic. It never used to bother me, and this is more of a recent development. Another thing that is anxiety provoking for me is having to be somewhere on a certain day at a certain time. If the appointment is two weeks away, I will obsess about it almost to the point of physical illness. My anxiety ramps up the day of the appointment, too. Whether it is a psychiatric appointment or having to be at a job. Jobs are so hard for me for this reason, but also I have a phobia of being constrained or restrained. I feel like when I am at a job that requires me to be there from 9-5 for example, I feel trapped. The time goes by so slowly. The anxiety is literally choking. It feels like there is an elephant sitting on my chest while I am there. I think that this phobia comes from being hospitalized on lock-down, and basically held against my will. I spent a night in a jail cell too while I was manic, and it was a horrific experience. Somewhat related, I always hated turtlenecks as a child and clothes in general. Could be because of the restraining nature of clothes.

I was asked to write a paper in high school about what I wanted to do when I grew up, and I had no answer except to be happy. That's all I really wanted, honestly. I chose psychology as my major because I wanted to understand why people thought and acted the way they did. I was confused how some people could act so strange, heartless, mean, angry, or whatever the situation may be. I wanted to see what made people tick, while others were not motivated by these same things. My plan was to continue to get my Ph.D., but I ran out of money, interest, and energy. I graduated in 2004, and I got sick in 2006 also. I was never much of a materialistic person, although sometimes I would go on spending sprees with the money I made (people with bipolar disorder tend to do this). I still just really want to be happy, and helping others has always made me feel that way. I always had a laid back attitude, and hardly ever got mad. I don't express my emotions very well and tend to keep things inside, usually resulting in a blowup of some sorts over something miniscule. I use poetry as an outlet sometimes. I still have never been in a fight to this day. Physically, anyway. My biggest fights have been against myself and my disorders.

While attending college, I had a live-in girlfriend that I thought I might marry someday. We dated about 3 years, but broke up before I graduated college. At that time, she got pregnant. I was devastated. I was 20. I'm not going to put all the blame on her, but the one time we had unprotected sex, she told me she couldn't get pregnant for all these different reasons, and I believed her. Within weeks, she had an abortion with my persuasion. I felt tricked and betrayed. I still think about it to this day and feel pretty guilty sometimes. I think of how old my child would be in the present day. I have a 12-year-old nephew that would have been about the same age as my child, if I had chosen to have him/her/it. I don't even know the right term to use. I was raised Catholic, and this was something that was definitely against my upbringing. I rationalize it sometimes by thinking that my ex and I could have never raised a child, and that child would have maybe had mental illness, which I wouldn't want to pass on or wish on anyone. I felt like there was no other option. It is one of my dark secrets that very few people know about. This girlfriend would show up later in life, but that is a different part of the story. During college, I was always on the go. If it wasn't work, it was schoolwork, if it wasn't school work, it was partying or giving attention to my girlfriend. I was barely sleeping. I would sometimes take Adderall to help me study, but mostly so I could stay awake and drink and party more. I was never prescribed it, but someone at school had extras and would give them to me if I asked, which wasn't that frequent.

I dated another woman who was studying to be an EMT. There was nothing serious about it. We worked at a sports bar together, and all we would do was get drunk and high together. It was fun, but it wasn't going anywhere. I lost contact with her eventually, and I found out about two weeks after we stopped seeing each other, she got pregnant. It scared the hell out of me, but luckily, it was not mine.

I graduated from the University of Dayton in 2004 and struggled to find a job. I graduated with a 2.95 GPA, which is pretty good all things considered, among the partying, working, and catatonic behavior. I used to be able to cram for exams, reading a hundred pages from a textbook in one night. Now, I can barely read one page from a book. I don't have the concentration or attention span anymore. The only thing I can watch on TV really is sports because I can't keep attention on any shows with a storyline or a plot. While attending the University of Dayton, I started to notice something odd. Every time I walked under street lamps, they would go out. I thought it was some sort of celestial or heavenly sign. That could have been a foreshadowing of my illness, but I joked about it, and it never impaired my functioning. The reality is these lamps are on timers or motion sensors, and it was mere coincidence.

I still lived in Dayton for another year before I bounced around from friend's to friend's houses because I didn't want to move back home and lose the independence I had. So, I went back to school and earned a real estate license. I had grand plans of being a real estate mogul like Donald Trump, but that didn't work out, yet anyway. These are called grandiose feelings, which are a symptom of bipolar disorder. You think you are superior and are going to succeed at a high level. You feel invincible. What they don't tell you in real estate school is the outrageous amount of money it takes to start up and be successful. The advice I was given from other agents and a broker was "Just get a credit card and charge everything and pay it off when you sell a house". I was not willing to do that and get more into debt. I got a job working at a pizza place I worked at in high school in my hometown. I was basically made a manager, and began working long hours. I began acting manic with the new job stress. I signed a lease to buy a house in my mania also. I was going to buy a new car. I couldn't afford any of it, but I thought I could. I guess this is where I tell you about the day that would forever change my life and the way I thought about everything.

11 DIAGNOSED

THIS IS WHERE THINGS ARE GOING TO GET A BIT FOGGY, AND I WILL PROBABLY HAVE to refer to my medical records at some point to be accurate. On July 31, 2006, (I will never forget the date, and always am very somber when it comes around each year) Sometimes I feel like it is a birthday though. I go through a range of feelings on this day. I am somber because the memory will never leave my mind, but grateful I am not in that place anymore. I went to the psychiatric unit of a hospital in Cincinnati. I was very paranoid, hearing voices, seeing things that weren't there, and demonstrating odd behaviors (all symptoms of bipolar disorder). I actually thought I heard the trumpets of angels calling to me. I had to lie down at my house to remain calm. I remember reading the Bible aloud in the waiting room. One of my brothers, who is as close to me as my father, noticed, and took me to the hospital. I was in such a frenzy that after I signed the papers for them to treat me; the nurses gave me a huge shot of some medicine and I went right to sleep for hours. I didn't realize I had just committed myself, and I tried to escape in my psychosis. About twelve security guards had to surround me before I would let them give me the shot. I found out later the drug was Geodon or Risperdal (I can't remember). I will tell you it was the best sleep of my life.

A doctor interviewed me and asked me questions like if I knew who the president and vice president were, and the day and date. I guess I was correct, but I don't remember. They asked me about all the drugs I have done, and I still remember the shocked looks on my parents' faces. It was all so surreal. It was like I was watching myself in a movie. I still get that feeling sometimes to this day. I think it is the brain's natural defense mechanism to withdrawal from a painful event. I spent 11 days there on a locked-down floor. I was hyper-religious, constantly reading the Bible and talking about God. I thought I could heal people and predict the future as well. I thought the end of the world was near. I almost jumped off a balcony because I thought I could fly. That's how strong the high of mania can be. Delusional thinking is also a symptom of bipolar disorder. This is what people in the psychiatric community call a "first break". Basically, when the symptoms of bipolar disorder become too intense to function, usually resulting in a hospitalization. I remember calling the governor of Ohio and leaving a message saying I was being held captive against my will. I think I also tried to order a pizza. They had a phone in the common area that the patients could use. Here is a statement from the hospital record:

"John Medl is a 24-year-old white male who endorses a history of paranoid behavior. He has no prior psychiatric diagnosis. His mother and brother brought him to University Hospital on July 31, 2006 because of his erratic behavior. Prior to admission, he broke into a car on July 29, 2006 because he believed that the CIA gave it to him. He also believed that he was receiving special messages from lottery tickets, television, and radio. He was smoking 10 to 20 joints a day" I would like to add that I wasn't smoking that much. When they interviewed me, I was psychotic, and really had no idea what was going on. And it continues," In University Hospital, the patient has been exhibiting extreme manic and psychotic symptoms, including elevated mood and labile affect. He has delusional thinking that he works for the CIA. He states that God is talking to him. He continues to be very grandiose. He has been irritable with staff on the unit. He has destroyed property and required emergency medication. He has been walking around with his backside exposed. He has decompensated since his admission.

Mr. Medl is currently suffering from Bipolar Affective Disorder, manic episode with psychotic features. His delusions and hallucinations and his irritable behavior represent a substantial risk to himself and others. It is the belief of this treatment team that the least restrictive, effective, and safe treatment option for Mr. Medl is as an inpatient in the locked down psychiatric unit. The patient will benefit from medication treatment, and the social and therapeutic milieu of the hospital."

I thought the CIA was following me and recruiting me. I thought there were microphones or "bugs" in my house to record what I was saying. I was getting messages through the TV. I could have sworn the TV changed channels by itself one time, but I probably sat on the remote control or some logical explanation. There was a gang in my neighborhood that I thought the CIA was rewarding me for exposing, which led to an arrest. In my mind, I was following clues and messages I was receiving that told me the CIA was going to give me a free car as a reward for helping to uncover this gang. I walked up to a complete stranger's car that was vacant and parked and got in. I was charged for trespassing and criminal damaging, but the charges were dropped on the account that I was not guilty by reason of insanity. Probably the best thing that could have happened to me. The police took me to jail, and I spent the night. I still remember how good the food tasted because I probably hadn't eaten in a day or so. Sauerkraut and hot dogs on white bread with water. I had to ask for the water I remember. In the morning, I saw a judge that specialized in mental illness. I was in complete psychosis, and have trouble remembering the details to this day. I know I was referred to an agency and a psychiatrist. I have received the excellent treatment I have received today in 2013 because of that arrest and hospitalization. Here is a poem that I wrote about describing that day and how I felt:

July 31, 2006

It was like lightning Struck my brain in two
A feeling I hope never happens to you.
Fueled by a combination
Of drugs and chemical failure
I never even saw it coming.
But in hindsight, they say things seem clearer
The teamwork of genetics, environment, and behavior.
A complete mental meltdown
Of someone competent and capable before
Never having a clue of what tests were in store.
I thought I would get better soon

Not months into years and more.
Confused, never in control
As the toxic cocktail took its toll
Crammed in a cell and then a bus to court
With total strangers, not knowing what I'd done Or where I was
But knowing it wasn't normal or fun
They had me sign some papers
That I couldn't focus to read
And plunged a needle deep in me
And gave me pills they said I'd need
They took me to a ward where I was greeted By shrieking vocal cords
They gave me a room, and a short tour
Life as I knew it, never more
A condition I guess they thought they could fix July thirty-first, two-thousand and six.

JOHN E MEDL

12 REVOLUTION

Around this time (not sure exactly) I felt a crazy amount of energy one night while I was on my front porch. I saw the American flag hanging off our house, and I ripped it off the house and began marching. I thought I was going to lead some kind of revolution. I marched with the flag waving from my house to a police station about 2 miles away. I felt like I could have run a marathon. Keep in mind, I was at least 400 pounds at the time, so you know the energy was at a high level. I walked into the police station and gave it to the dispatcher working at the time. I think my mindset was that I was giving the flag to the police in appreciation for their service. One of my best friends saw me in this mania around this time also. She thought I was on cocaine because I was talking so fast. I wasn't making sense, and I just kept ordering drinks. I had no control over what I was doing. My body was the vehicle, and my brain was the driver.

I forgot to mention that I starting dating a girl around 2005, and we rarely spent time apart. We would just sit around her apartment, smoke pot and/or drink beer, play games, watch TV, and eat, and that was enough for us. We went out every once in a while, but not much. She worked for a big time company, and she was consumed by it, but we still managed to hang out a lot. I never really thought it was going anywhere. The biggest clue was when I met her parents and they scolded me like a child for getting up from the dinner table without asking to be excused. A little too uptight for my taste. She had a saying she would write on any card she gave me or present. It was "amor vincit omnia", which means "love conquers all" in Latin. She even had a watch engraved with that saying on it. I still have it, but I don't know why. I couldn't care less where it ends up. Very soon after being released from the hospital, she dumped me. Pretty hypocritical, if you ask me.

13 EXHAUSTION

From August 2006 to September 2007, I slept almost all day and all night. My couch was my favorite place to sleep, and I remember watching out of the large window above the couch watching life go by. Here is a poem that describes how I felt about that:

Quilted Sofa

Padded checkers and rings
Hold my see-saw feelings
Tragedy, triumph, good, and bad
The best rest I've ever had.
Once glued, now improved
I got back everything
I used to groggily wish for.
Now I seem to be
Trapped in my own clarity.
Truths that will haunt me for years, and fears, dried up tears
Steered by sanity now, but how?
No better time to start than now
Forcing me to stand pat

A curse worse than a black cat Labels by faces, replaces
All the old thoughts about myself.
But I know who and what I am Like it or not
Do you really think my soul forgot?

Here is a quote I really like that explains how I feel about the difference between my old self and my medicated, non-manic self:

"I compare myself with my former self, not with others. Not only that, I tend to compare my current self with the best I have been, which is when I have been mildly manic. When I am my present "normal" self, I am far removed from when I have been my liveliest, most productive, most intense, most outgoing and effervescent. In sort, for myself, I am a hard act to follow."

Kay Redfield Jamison, An Unquiet Mind: A Memoir of Moods and Madness

14 ADMITTED AGAIN

I never thought I would be able to function again. A very depressing feeling. The doctors explained they medicated me to "bring me down" from my mania. This was a time where I almost gave up and gained over 100lbs from eating all the time and being sedentary. I slept at least 18 hours a day. The medication warned that it may cause weight gain, so I figured if it was going to happen anyway, I would eat anything and everything I wanted. In retrospect, not such a great idea. So, I guess this brings me to 2007. I got a job at a sandwich shop and excelled delivering food and managing, too. The owner wanted to send me to Chicago to be an assistant general manager. I thought I would be there forever.

On June 13, 2008, I was admitted again to a hospital for being in a manic episode. A lot of things were happening in my life like the job stress and long hours, my mom having her hip replaced, and a friend of mine from high school and college died in a boating accident. Stress and loss of a loved one, or loss in general, almost certainly will trigger a manic episode, and it did. I was on a 24 hour watch because of my out-of-control behavior. I am referring to my medical records for the next set of dates. I pulled the fire alarm because I wanted help to escape. The pleasant things I remember were that we had a little Bible study group, and we would read the Bible and pray every day. There were about 25 people on the floor, males and females. There was a refrigerator full of apple juice and wedged cheese that there was an endless supply of for the patients. They had a lot of board games, support groups, and even arts and crafts. I was resistant to participate in any of this at first because I was very paranoid of everyone and wanted to be released immediately. I wasn't exactly thrilled to be there, either. Eventually, I calmed down and started to interact with the other patients.

I remember one night I woke up about 3AM, and I thought I had been flown to the Vatican to meet the Pope. I would wake up at these odd hours and process down the halls holding the Bible up like I was at Mass. I also remember thinking I was Jesus reincarnated at some point. I thought a major earthquake was going to hit the US, so I requested a printout of all the major fault lines in the US. There was never an earthquake in the US, but one happened in China. I thought my predictive abilities were just a little off, and I had misinterpreted the "signs". I was over analyzing everything. I was using cryptology on everything from soda cans to the microwave. I remember thinking the microwave and thermostat were just cover-ups that actually controlled all of the patients' minds.

I was released on June 16th with all new meds and I hit a parked car because I thought I was getting messages from my stereo to lose my license. Specifically, my stereo read "protect", and in my delusional world, that meant lose my license. I think I thought that I needed to be protected from the outside world, so I could accomplish some grand feat. I lost my license, but criminal charges were dropped after I told my lawyer and the judge I was the "chosen one". I don't know exactly what I meant, but it warranted another not guilty by reason of insanity. I know it doesn't make sense, but it feels like it does when you are in an episode like that. I was released on June 19. I was sending emails to the White House, criticizing President Bush. Nothing wrong with that, really, but I thought the government was going to come find me.

On June 20, I called the life squad because of an anxiety attack and was taken to the hospital and released.

On June 23, I called the life squad again for the same reason, but never hospitalized. My meds got changed again, and I was a little more stable. I had to cut my hours from about 60 to 20 and began sleeping most of the time again. This is also when panic disorder was added to my diagnoses. All the while I was battling with Social Security to be granted disability benefits, but to this day, I get denied over and over. I am still in the process 7 years later. This is where it gets blurry.

I know I quit that job because I was very paranoid and demonstrated erratic, manic behavior. It was a shame because I liked the job; I was good at it, and the owner and staff liked me. Between my symptoms and the side effects of my medication, I could not function even on the lowest of levels.

15 WEIGHT

The next date I really remember is September 11. Weight. I was 591 lbs. I used to weigh myself on a scale meant for measuring large loads of scrap metal, and the red glowing numbers that were on the meter are burned into my brain permanently. I got down to 447 lbs. by eating a very low-fat diet. I didn't even have to exercise, just eat better. In June 2012, I was about 485 lbs. In May 2013, I am about 525 pounds. A lot of the medication that people, then in 2009, when I decided I was going to lose with mental illness are prescribed cause weight gain, but not necessarily everyone. In October 2009, my sister got married, and I wore a suit with size 72 pants. I now wear a size 56. Not really that important, but I was proud of myself, and I think this confidence propelled me to be more social and outgoing, like my old self. One of the constant depressing things is that I always compared myself to my "old self" that could handle a job and stress, and had fun all the time. It takes a lot of time and therapy to get over that line of thinking, which I still struggle with. I most likely will never be as productive as I was while in high school and college, and accepting that as a reality is a tough pill to swallow, no pun intended.

I have been overweight my whole life. I was almost eleven pounds when I was born, and I never stopped growing. I was almost six feet tall in the eighth grade. My mom used to have to alter all my school or sports uniforms so that they would fit me. I had trouble fitting into the desks at school, too. I never had much confidence with the opposite sex for that reason. I always thought that all women only liked skinny boys, and that they would find me disgusting. Later in life, I learned that wasn't true, but as a child, I was very embarrassed. People loved to feed me. I would get extra portions in the school lunch line. I would eat dinner at home, and then go to a friend's house, only to have his/her parents feed me again. I didn't know any better. I ate almost everything available. In fact, my mom was overweight my whole childhood as well, until she lost over 100 pounds within the last five years or so. She is somewhat of a "health nut" now, but she didn't know any better when I was younger and she was preparing meals.

Mental illness can be very embarrassing and can break down your confidence. It was like one day; I was fully functioning, and the next day, I was in the hospital. The family and friends you had before the hospital knew you to be a certain person and then they see you psychotic in a hospital. I was lucky that some of my best friends came to visit. My parents would sneak me in my favorite Mexican food too.

It felt like the rug got pulled out from under me, and I am still traumatized and haunted by it to this day. My whole line of thought and goals and beliefs changed. When I felt better, I started to live in the moment more, and it was hard for me to make long-term goals or plans. I still carry on that way. After things like this happen, you are constantly worried it is going to happen again. I am grateful for every day that I get, so the notion of thinking about retirement or any sort of long-term goals is not possible for me. The best days are when I forget about my past, but it doesn't happen often. This is probably why I self-medicated with alcohol. To forget. Basically, the same reason others drink, I think. To forget about your worries and responsibilities for a little while. But, in addition, alcohol made my symptoms disappear. This is very reinforcing as you could imagine. Bipolar disorder can be very cyclical; you are symptomatic, so you drink because you are on Cloud 9. Your symptoms disappear for a little while. Then, the symptoms come back and the process may repeat all over again.

In 2009, I was focused on losing weight, and not much else. I know I didn't see my friends for a while because I was so ashamed at how large I was. When I started to lose weight, I started to gain confidence and be social again. I had fun just like any person in his/her twenties. Alcohol or marijuana was almost always involved, but that was familiar territory for me. No one ever forced me to do anything. It was just what we did while we were hanging out. I guess it added a little variety to whatever we were doing those nights. I tried my hand at various jobs, but would eventually quit either because of conflicts with co-workers or I would begin to get symptomatic, and the job would be too much.

16 LIVE, AND LEARN

Presently, I do not have a typical job. I receive $115 a month cash and $200 a month in food stamps from the state of Ohio. I also have Medicaid. I do market research and eBay for money, and then I usually take that money to gamble, with some success. I have gambled since I was a child really at church festivals, which is acceptable once a year at that age. I got into it heavier in college and began to play poker. I went to Canada to gamble at a casino when I was 19 because back then, the gambling and drinking age was only 18. I went with one of my exes, and we won about 2500 dollars on the first day. That made for a great trip because our budget was around 600 bucks. The legal age is 21 now, and you need a passport. That wasn't the case when I went. When I turned 21, I started going to bars and the casino with some frequency. I enjoyed both very much. I am in a poker club too, with a bunch of great people that I enjoy playing cards with to this day. Some may think I have a problem because I gamble so frequently, but it's hard for me to admit that. I just think of it as entertainment and keeping my mind occupied. I just figure if I lose, I will cut back on some other activity. I would never steal or sell a house or anything to get a "fix". I think the people who don't have a gambling spirit are really the ones that don't understand. For instance, my parents are not gamblers, and stress out over me losing as little as thirty dollars. To me, that is not a big deal, and definitely worth the price for entertainment. What would I do with the money otherwise? I'm not materialistic. I don't like shopping. I would probably spend that money at a bar or on alcohol, so I am trading one vice for another, I guess.

I am the administrator for a Facebook page devoted to helping the mentally ill and inform others about mental illness. There are almost 300 members. I don't get paid for it, but it is rewarding nonetheless. My paternal grandfather passed away May 4, 2012. We were never that close, and I didn't realize I would miss him so much. It got me thinking about losing more people close to me and ramped up my anxiety. It made me think of my own mortality as well. He served in WWII and had a military burial. I could not attend the wake or the funeral on account of my anxiety disorders. Once again, another loss in my life. I think this set off a bout of mania that ended with my last hospitalization that was June 10 , 2012. My parents were at Mass on Sunday, like they always do, and for some reason, I couldn't sit still. My mind was going 1000 miles per hour, and I couldn't quit pacing. My arms were tingling, and I thought I was having a heart attack. I thought I was going to die. I couldn't speak either, so my mom had to talk to a doctor on-call, and he advised we go to the hospital. I was transported in an ambulance to a hospital about fifteen miles away. That was the longest car ride of my life. I had on an oxygen mask that helped regulate my breathing, which was helping me slightly. All I could think about was all the people that I never got to say goodbye to. I was convinced I was having a heart attack and was going to die. I spent about six hours at the hospital, and nothing was done for me. When I felt the panic come on originally, I took a Xanax and a Klonopin. They had no effect. The doctor described it as "my brain took over my body". That's a pretty scary thought, but not far-fetched. Your brain is the control center for everything. I guess I just had never heard it put that way before. I didn't like that there was basically nothing I could have done. I have been sober ever since. On July 13, 2012, I relapsed and had about 8 beers. I felt terrible in the morning, and I don't think it is really worth it. I equate having alcohol to drink as an option as a sense of normalcy. I feel restrained if I don't think I can drink like a lot of my friends. The reality is, I am a different person with different reactions and effects to alcohol. I may not be able to drink at all, or very rarely. I was terrified to take a drink because I did not want to end up in the hospital again. I have reduced my caffeine intake dramatically as well, but lately, that is increasing as well. I haven't smoked pot in months. I feel like there is no other option. I can do everything in my power to get better, or continue to aggravate my disorders and probably end up in the hospital again. A hospitalization is always a reality for me, whether I follow my treatment plan or not. By the way, I have always followed my treatment plan, and have never missed one dose of medicine or appointment in 7 years. My most recent appointment on July 18, 2012, I could not attend physically because of my disorders. All five of my anxiety disorders can work with each other and at the same time. My doctor was nice enough to have a phone conference with me to see how I was doing. My doctor is three miles away at the most, and even that distance is too much to handle for me. He told me that if I know I will have a panic attack doing an activity, don't do it. This is against my nature because I always want to try to overcome obstacles and challenges at all costs, but I need to realize that I simply cannot beat panic disorder, or any of the other ones. All I can do is damage control and look out for my own personal well-being. Being so compliant probably hurts my case for Social Security Disability. They want someone who is not compliant. I have been 100% compliant. At any point and time, the chemicals in my brain can literally take over my body and cause a relapse. It's not a great feeling. I am constantly assessing my thought processes to see if I am okay, to the point of an obsession. People with bipolar disorder are strongly discouraged to have caffeine, alcohol, or any recreational drugs, so I am staying away for now the best I can. The possibility of a relapse is very possible and real, but all I can do is try my best.

Some time between 2009 and 2010, I dated a girl who was studying to be a nurse. She had a young daughter, and we all got along. She has a big heart and a great personality, and we still talk to this day. We eventually broke up because I got too attached. People with bipolar disorder tend to do this, but I may have especially been attached because she was the first woman I had been with since my first hospitalization. I loved that she liked me for who I was. I was still very heavy, but she didn't mind. She liked me for what I had to offer on the inside, and I respect that. I also respected her for raising her daughter alone after a failed marriage. She was the person that sort of re-socialized me back into the world. We went to the zoo, and on a bunch of mini adventures that helped my confidence grow back.

In August 2011, I got back together with my college sweetheart I mentioned earlier in the story. Big mistake. While we were apart for 8 years or so, she was diagnosed with Multiple Sclerosis, a horrible neurological disorder. She was a recovering drug addict, and she didn't contact me until she was clean because she knew she would have had no chance with me otherwise. Again, I thought I might marry her. I basically moved in with her, and we got along okay until the end. She kicked me out of her apartment in January 2012, and I moved back in on a full-time basis with my parents. I feel like I was manic then, too. I was constantly running errands and doing chores. It was stressful to be with someone with such a horrible illness. She was always in pain, and she couldn't go out much or enjoy herself very often. Most of the time, we just sat in her apartment. We hardly ever spent time apart. Then, like I said, we broke up in January. I think I was undersexed and wanted to relive the good times we had while I was in college. Definitely a bad decision on my part. To her credit, I probably wouldn't have graduated without her financial contributions to the bills while I was in college. Life had been hard on her since then, and we were both different people. You live and you learn.

17 MEDICINAL HAZE

I HAVE GIVEN YOU A PRETTY GOOD BACKGROUND OF MY LIFE TO THIS POINT, BUT what do I go through on a daily basis? How do I feel most of the time? Well, it's no picnic, but I try to keep it in a perspective that there are others who have it much worse. I only sleep three hours at night, and wake up usually with racing thoughts about what I have to do that day. I wake up about 3AM. I usually take two naps during daylight hours near my medication times. I am anxious most of the day. I obsess about death and dying; my own, as well as others. At times, I have had suicidal idealization, but no attempts. I have trouble driving a car, or even riding in one sometimes. Appointments are the worst for me. I obsess about them to the point of physical sickness. If I have to be somewhere on a certain day at a certain time, my anxiety is almost unbearable. I pace a lot, and I have a hard time sitting still. I would love to be able to concentrate enough to read or watch a movie, but sports is really all my attention can handle. I obsessively check my email, eBay, and Facebook, probably 50 times a day. I am constantly counting or running numbers in my head about making money or the probability of this or that. I constantly check the clock, whether because it is near my med times, or just out of habit. I feel every little bodily sensation I have, usually pain. I worry that there is something physically wrong with me. I have constant headaches, and I get dizzy a lot. I make a lot of lists, from what I want to accomplish that day or in the future. It could be to organize something too. I have odd sleeping times, and my meds make me feel sedated a lot. I go through cycles of being wide awake and anxious to near comatose. Here is a poem that describes how my medicine makes me feel sometimes:

Medicinal Haze

I wake up in a medicinal haze
Left over from the night
And remember all the happy days
And all the ways I used to cope.
Those were times filled with hope
Now instead of being free,
The doctors pump me full of dope.
With the stroke of his pen
He can control my behavior
Like some holier-than-thou savior
Saving me from myself
Maybe I did need help
Maybe I'll be better off
Some people hear disorder
And think it can be cured
Like a cold or cough
But it will never go away, never will
At least the drugs keep me still
Too still sometimes, more like a zombie
I guess the challenge is
Finding a balance between the new and the old me.

18 MENTAL FOG

I AM IN A FOG A LOT. IT'S LIKE WATCHING MYSELF IN A MOVIE. I THINK THE technical term is depersonalization. I think it is my brain giving up on reality for a period of time because it is always in overdrive. It is almost comparable to sleepwalking. I can be looking someone dead in the face, trying my best to pay attention, and I don't comprehend what he/she is saying. It is so frustrating because I really do care what he/she is saying, but I may come off as if I am ignoring them. Also, when in mania or psychosis, a similar thing happens, but to a greater extent. When I get manic or have been through psychosis, I had no idea what was going on, but I could remember bits and pieces after the fact. Such an odd feeling.

After seven years of trying, I was approved for disability in October 2013. Yes, the money is nice, so I am not such a financial burden on my parents, but the validation was the best part. I almost fell over when I heard the news. After all, the hospital and doctor visits. After all, the medication changes. After all the fighting. To me, the approval is saying, "We recognize that your illness is real and debilitating. You are not lazy. Your condition is too severe to work right now." I would give all the money back if it meant I could live a normal lifestyle and work a traditional job and support myself; however, that's not the reality of the situation. At least for now. I never rule out the possibility that I will get better. I want to be able to handle being in a crowd, so maybe I could enjoy a rock concert or sporting event. I want to be able to travel further than a few miles from my house. I want many things—simple things to most. I know that giving up will get me nowhere, so working hard is my only option.

I really try to improve a little every day, but sometimes I get knocked back a few pegs. I have to realize this is going to happen, and I have to dust myself off and keep trying. This is easier said than done when I am fighting disappointment on top of my brain's faulty brain chemistry.

19 FIGHTING EVERY DAY

Current Update---> It is August 2014. Not much has changed. My last update from above (October 2013) pretty much applies. I am still fighting every day, both my illness and my weight. I have gained about forty pounds. My doctor thinks I may have Post Traumatic Stress Disorder from being in the hospital as well. Basically, I start to panic at random times when I am near a hospital or I might have flashbacks of all the times I have spent in them. Claustrophobia has been remov.ed as part of my diagnosis, and I have gone from five prescriptions to three (Cogentin and Xanax were eliminated). If I ever need medicinal help for a panic attack, I just have to take extra Klonopin. The final part of the book will be included, which is all my poetic works, in no particular order. After reading the book, it should be pretty easy to understand where my material comes from. I have been a published poet at maverickmagazine.com for many years. Over 12,000 people have read the poems I have published. Most of the poems I am including in this book never got to publishing, due to my lack of motivation. I am available through email at johnmedl7@gmail.com, if anyone has questions or comments. You can also friend me on Facebook if you so choose. My Facebook page for the mentally ill now has 401 members. I hope you have enjoyed my story and learned something. Thank you for your time.

20 I GIVE IT ALL I'VE GOT

When I feel down,
I go back to that place.
The needles and doctors
My mind can't erase.
My concerned friends and family
Who came to visit,
And how my entire life
Is wrapped up in it.
It's everything to me.
It's what drives me to be
A good person and friend.
A success story.
I was down on the mat,
But I got up.
I don't know how or why.
I could have easily given up
And kissed my future goodbye.
I must not be done yet
Or else it would have ended.
My dreams aren't gone,

They just got suspended.
I gave it everything I had
I reached down deep
The memories still haunt me Even in sleep.
When I have a bad day,
It can always be worse
The curse of making it through.
I give it all I've got
In everything I do.

JOHN E. MEDL

21 PAIN FOR MILES

Behind the laughter and the smiles
There is pain for miles
I've cried so many times
Pleading it will stop
It always seems to
When it wants to.
Most people don't know what makes me tick
I don't even know if I do
Maybe some day I will find out
How and why I got sick.
Maybe because I used to take life for granted
I never appreciated the little things
I just went about going through the motions
Never noticing anything surrounding the path I was on.
Most people have never seen me cry
I hide my emotions well
Every day is as big as a mountain
But you will probably not be able to tell.
My life's an open book
For everyone to read

I like it that way
Nothing to hide
Everything to explain
Like why sometimes
I prefer the rain.
Or why I value the company of friends so much
Or how my thoughts got out of touch
I reach down deep every minute of every day
I try my best to get through them
As hard as they are
But at least I got a poem.

JOHN E. MEDL

22 STANDING TALL

My head is pounding
And my mind won't quit
The hospital and medications
All because of it.
The sirens scream
Getting closer and closer
Until they are clear as can be
You can imagine my terror
When I knew they were coming for me.
Laid out on a stretcher
Gasping for air
I wanted to be anywhere but there.
Every second felt like ages
And not a thousand pages
Could capture
How it has come to this.
Never a day goes by
When I don't obsess about it all
But through every single battle
At least I've stood tall.

JOHN E. MEDL

23 LEGACY

My brain is on fire and my mind won't quit
Sometimes, I get sick of all of it.
I fight and I fight, but sometimes it's not enough
I just want to be known as tough.
I have a sense of humor to keep it light
I just want to do what's right.
My purpose is to make people smile and laugh
In that, I firmly believe
You can have all the money and all that comes with it.
I just want to leave a legacy of great stories.
That's what I want to achieve.
That others will commit
To their memories and have a lasting impression in their hearts.
At one time, I was torn apart.
I keep getting up and sometimes I don't know why or how
But I'm a lot closer to knowing now.

JOHN E. MEDL

24 I CARRY IT AROUND

As I've gotten older
I carry around the hurt
As a chip on my shoulder.
I carry it around as a fire inside
When it starts burning
There's nowhere to hide.
I carry it around
As a weight on my back
Sometimes I can't shake it
Sometimes I look back.
I carry it around
Like concrete in my shoes
Hard to move forward
But refusing to lose.
Making giant steps
Stumble by stumble
Sometimes it's too much
But it keeps me humble.
A mind that doesn't stop
Cranking and cranking

It keeps me occupied
And it keeps me thanking
My lucky stars
For what could have been.
How it could be.
I focus more on that
Than how it should be.

JOHN E. MEDL

25 I'LL NEVER FORGET

And in my darkest hour You had a kind word
My brain wasn't working
But I somehow still heard.
I remember your smiles
When my memory was lost
I remember the visits
At such a cost.
I remember your concern
At every single step
I remember how sad you were
Even while I slept.
I'll never forget
When you gave me your heart
Even when our souls
Were miles apart.
Even then
I still never forgot
All the love you gave
Towards the story, and the plot I'm here today
Doing pretty well

Mostly because of you
And partly from going through hell.
There will still be those that don't believe
Everything I say
I've had some awful moments
And I still count the days.
I've learned a great deal
About life and about myself
I've taken all your acts
And placed them on a shelf
Any given moment
I can reach back in time
And remember what you gave me
Truly sublime.

JOHN E. MEDL

26 HOW MANY NIGHTS DO I HAVE LEFT?

Many times a day I wonder
How many nights I have left
I wonder if I would even want to know.
I wonder if I am living right
When the world tells me 'no'.
I wonder if Fate will smile kindly on me
And let me be around
I wonder if I have done enough work
Before they lay me in the ground.
Or let the wind take my ashes to the sea
That's really the only place I wish to be.
I try to imagine how far the stars are away
And if I will get to see one up close some day.
I only know how to live one way—
The simplest way
I possibly can.
And at the same time
Leaving the Earth a good man.

JOHN E. MEDL

27 THE GRAVEYARD

Only when you've stared death in the face
And survive
Only then are you truly alive.
Live like it is your last day
Don't make it something you just say.
I know this from experience
It's not some theoretical idea to me
I consider it a blessing to be
Reminded so soon of my mortality.
Some sail through life, no worries, and that's great
But this is not a lesson you want to learn late.
Let me be an example
And lend your ear
The struggles I have had,
I hope you are never near.
And to you, I say good luck
Painting the canvas of life
And I hope your days are filled
With not a bit of strife
But if life deals you an altering hitch

I can only wish
You find the strength to carry on
May all your troubles be short,
and your days long.
If life's so easy
And not so hard
Why do I believe
They are dancing in the graveyard?
Laughing when we drive past
With convincing looks it will all last
Stress and and blur our thoughts
At least the dead are never lost
And never feel the need for greed
No violence or destruction
Not to ever have to bleed
Or the pressure to succeed.
If you deem these thoughts bizarre
Try looking out from the graveyard.

JOHN E. MEDL

28 THE HEAVENS

I hope I soar into the heavens
Far above the sky.
I know I'll see all the angels
That too early, passed us by.
I want to meet all the saints
And ask them a lot of questions
Maybe over a nice dinner
And talk about the people I want to mention.
Maybe it will be an ocean
And I'll fall into the darkest depths
A peaceful place of silence
Filled with tears we all wept.
But maybe I'll be sent to
Hell The fire and smoky air—
A place for only a few
But I think I've already been there.

JOHN E. MEDL

29 MAKING LEMONADE

In that place
All I feel is fear
And thoughts about death
Are near.
When it is through
I just want to cry
Another step backwards
Telling myself all I can do is try.
Enough to bring a big man
To his knees
And pray for it to be over
Begging for the end, please!
A terror so potent
Minutes feel like days
Feelings so strong
My ego always pays
I never know when it will come
I just know I'm grateful when it's done
I sometimes wish I were the only one.
I just want someone to tell me it's okay

I just want the words to help convey
How awful the panic really can be
If you could only see
How crippling it really is
How painful and strong
Not matter how short, it always seems long
And I always feel wronged
What did I do?
I try to be a good person
And do what's right
I try and work hard
And I'm thankful at night
I know deep down it's not my fault
But I always retrace my actions
And my past deeds
Even though I know
I can't go back
I think if I do enough good
I can cover my tracks.
But the fact is,
Nothing I did
Has anything to do with me now
For some reason, I have been chosen
To make lemonade somehow.
I don't want your pity
That's not the point
I can't say enough
To get anyone to feel how terrible it can be
I wouldn't wish it on my worst enemy

JOHN E. MEDL

30 JUST A PARK

The sycamore and oak trees
Bow and wave to greet me
And immediately their presence
Makes me feel at peace.
One of my sanctuaries
I've been visiting for years
Not one tall building or store around
Just the trees and me
The rustling of leaves, the only sound.
Just a quiet spot to simply think
That's all I was really after
No music, conversation, or laughter.
No one to judge me by my fame or wealth
Or to criticize and scrutinize my health
Fields and woody statues
As far as I can see
At this place, in this time,
I can't think of a place I'd rather be.

JOHN E. MEDL

31 UNTOUCHED

My eyes pick out crosses everywhere
From just regular, everyday things.
I see light flashes
And I don't know if they are really there.
I dream about people far in the past
Some dreams I wish were over fast
And some I wish would last.
I've been wide awake
And I didn't know where I was.
I used to tempt the Fates
Just because.
Most of the time, I'm just sort of 'there'
Not blissful but not particularly down either.
When I'm down,
it's the worst I've ever felt
But when I feel alive,
it's the best I've ever been.
Even when crying, at least it's a feeling
What I'm implying
Is that there are very tall hills and deep, dark, holes

Sometimes I'm embarrassed when my story is told.
But as age creeps up
Talking does more good than harm
Most are inspired
But some will always be alarmed.
A boat I have elected myself the captain
Attempting to steer ashore
The turmoil rising from below
The thunder pounding from above I am surrounded—
And I am supposed to find land?
The sea sees no penalty when chaotic
But woe to the mind when disturbed
Shaken off course—
With an earthquake off the charts
My whole functioning without the parts
Vital to survive and succeed.
A persistent bleed from my heart through my skin
So the heart is where I shall begin
To repair what has failed for years.
I have survived typhoons and tidal waves countless times I have crossed uncrossable lines
And disaster has gratefully let me prepare
For the misfortunes fortunate enough to plague me.
An easy task for they have seen stronger
But they will not weaken me a minute longer
Unknown, a formidable enemy clenches his fist
Executing his plans down the list.
The resilient may at first seem meek
The strong at first weak
But victory hides in the end
A winner wins at the finish of a race
Not the beginning, soon to be erased.
Others are happy just to place
But winners all the same.
A spirit deserving of a name
But no one word could do justice

Call it a spark or flame
They wonder whom to blame
For these countless, relentless tries—
The sun dies, the wind cries, and the sea subsides.
You will not hold me back, turbulent sea
For my soul will set fire
As the kindling lay before me.
Fuel for my motor
A motivation unseen by woe or worry
A whirlwind of fury—
Let it strike down
Those who dare subjugate me
Under an umbrella of expectations
That even God would fall short.
But I will not, I refuse
To let abuse—abuse me
I remain untouched and will forever be.

JOHN MEDL

32 POSER FRIENDS

Self-reflection has revealed
An ejection of delusions and false hope.
A more quiet way to cope
Than screaming what I really think of you.
You are the weaker link of a chain now broken
Not even a sentimental token am I left with
A revelation freed from a dark hole
Like a mole, poking its head out for air
Far away in some hand-me-down chair
If you only knew what you lost
But that's just my perception
No better than the rest, no exception
You are no better friend than I am to you
Never have been
I'd like to cram, all your lies back in your mouth
One by one, 'til you choke
Our "friendship" was just a horrible, cruel joke.
Thanks, once again, poser friend
Your memory will never make me laugh again
I must have run out of what you wanted

Or you would still be around.
All I can say, and I hope you take with you
As penance for all your faults
Locked down tight in mental vaults
I could delicately unravel
But I would rather see you crack and explode
Blow the doors off, and the landing won't be soft, no loft Smack against a wall
I could watch you fall over and over again
I saw the end from afar
And now I'm glad to see who you really are.
You piece of nothing, trash on the street
Rancid and sour
And in your final hours, you can explore
The dark abysses you created
And I'm elated to see you doing so poorly
I used to be concerned, surely
When you were someone else...

JOHN MEDL

33 QUILTED SOFA

Padded checkers and rings
Hold my see-saw feelings
Tragedy, triumph, good, and bad
The best rest I've ever had.
Once glued, now improved
I got back everything
I used to groggily wish for.
Now I seem to be
Trapped in my own clarity.
Truths that will haunt me for years, and fears, dried up tears
Steered by sanity now, but how?
No better time to start than now
Forcing me to stand pat
A curse worse than a black cat
Labels by faces, replaces
All the old thoughts about myself.
But I know who and what I am
Like it or not
Do you really think my soul forgot?

JOHN E. MEDL

34 MY MIND IS ON REPLAY

My mind is on replay
Day after day
I saw a man strapped to his bed
Nurses approaching with needles Inhuman cries and moans
He was trapped inside his head
Every day I think about being dead
Going on seven years
It gets old really fast
The same old fears
My mind is on replay
Day after day
I take medication for some relief
I wish there were some other way
My mind is on replay
Day after day
My thoughts race in circles
The acts in some strange play
My mind is on replay
Day after day
I talk myself out of giving up

But sometimes I stray
My mind is on replay
Day after day
I have to check the clocks
To make sure time is okay
I don't check the locks
Those don't bother me much
I do check my own thoughts
To make sure I'm in touch
My mind is on replay
Day after day
Sometimes I get frustrated
Recovery seems so far away
My mind is on replay
Day after day
I have to write it all down
And put it on display
It helps to express some things In a creative way
My mind is on replay
Day after day

JOHN E. MEDL

35 I DON'T NEED YOUR SYMPATHY

I don't need your sympathy.
I'll make some coffee
And have a cup with me.
Our roads crossed for some reason
Time don't matter or the season
But I don't need your sympathy.
We can talk until our tongues go dry
And if we need to
We can wipe each other's eyes.
I just love your company
But I don't need your sympathy.
I'll light a smoke while you're talking
And I'll listen the best I can
I want to hear your point of view
And all the things that make up you
But I don't need your sympathy.
I don't have close to all the answers
But maybe we have some common ground.
I just want to make you feel better
I know pain and I know healing

But I don't need your sympathy.
Our talk is over now and it's time to go
Maybe we can do this again
If I say I am your friend,
I will be one to the end,
But I don't need your sympathy.

JOHN E. MEDL

36 THERE IS HOPE

I lose my mind from time to time
But I always seem to find it
I sometimes get excited about the future
But my past looms right behind it
Pain that pity and recovery can't resolve
An assortment of memories involved
And plans that never blossomed.
But if anyone thinks for one second
I will give up my hopes and dreams
Just to spite the daily screams
There's just some things I can't repress
I try to give my all and nothing less.

JOHN E. MEDL

37 WHEN THE SUNSHINE WENT AWAY

As I watched clouds explode
And stars collide
The sky swallowed itself in submission
An event for no one's eyes
But that night
With my mind's permission
I witnessed the grim possibility of the future.
The catastrophic, violent images
Disturbed me enough to retreat
And run from the Creator and Destroyer
No hope for success, the inevitable demise
But that's not what our state implies
And when greed, power, and money combine
They will leave nothing behind.
As soon as I woke
I pleaded to the silence
To never let me see the day
When the sunshine goes away

JOHN E. MEDL

38 NEVER BREAK

Usually when my mind is racing
I write my best
But today my mind is taking a rest.
Not thinking much at all
Unusual for me.
A sense of peace and calm
Bathed in mirth and security.
My thoughts are not frantic
Unusual for me.
Feeling pretty fantastic
But never to the highest degree.
Not too sluggish
Or nerves standing on end.
No negative thinking
And realizing I just bend
Never break.
If I could only find which road to take.

JOHN E. MEDL

39 WHO YOU WERE MEANT TO BE

Most of all I wish you joy
Happiness beyond measure
Infinite pleasure
And satisfaction with your life.
Only you are you
And it is who you were meant to be
Don't wish to be someone else
You were made perfectly.
If you should fall,
pick yourself up
And I wish for you,
an overflowing cup.
Try to be kind and increasingly wise
There isn't much else
As much as I can surmise.
I want for you the very best
And I mean that more than you know
I hope you find a blissful place
A respite, in your mind, you can go.
Don't spend too much time

On sadness and despair
Seconds are precious
And there are no flowers there.
Pick up the pieces, one by one
Until you feel whole
Nothing will ever be perfect
Not everything you can control.
Try to be your best
Every single day
Show the world your greatness
In every single way.

JOHN E. MEDL

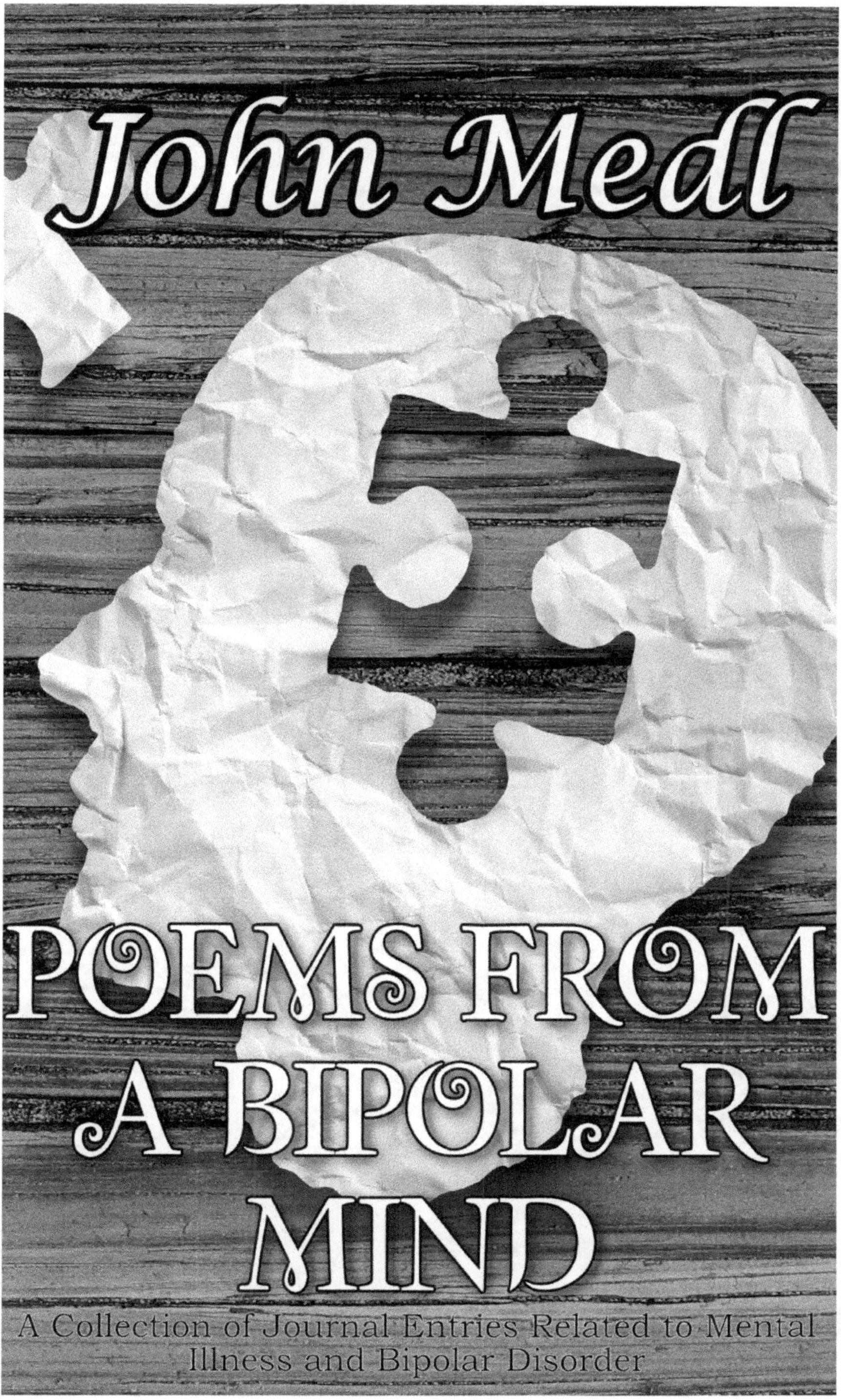
John Medl
POEMS FROM
A BIPOLAR
MIND
A Collection of Journal Entries Related to Mental
Illness and Bipolar Disorder

I want to dedicate this book to my parents, family, and friends who have never left my side through my battles with mental illness. I also want to dedicate this book to the millions of people who suffer from mental illness around the world. I hope I have done well in being the voice of the suffering.

INTRODUCTION

This is the second book I have written. My first book is titled, "Millions Like Me: My Struggle with Mental Illness". That's my whole life story up until 2013. This book is a book of poetry, with commentary mixed in. For clarity purposes, I wanted to give you a brief introduction. I have been writing poems since grade school. I am now 35 years old. These are all the poems I could find. There is no real order to any of the poems. I hope that my commentary will help clarify what I was thinking and feeling at the time. In 2006, I was diagnosed with bipolar disorder with psychotic features. Since 2006, the doctors have added Post Traumatic Stress Disorder, Generalized Anxiety Disorder/Panic Disorder, Obsessive Compulsive Disorder, agoraphobia, and claustrophobia. For the full story, reference my first book. I wanted a book completely devoted to the poetic arts. Just as with my first book, I hope this book leaves a positive, lasting impression on the readers.

1 NAVIGATING TROUBLED WATERS

A boat I have elected myself the captain
Attempting to steer ashore
The turmoil rising from below
The thunder pounding from above
I am surrounded—
And I am supposed to find land?
The sea sees no penalty when chaotic
But woe to the mind when disturbed
Shaken off course—
With an earthquake off the charts
My whole functioning without the parts
Vital to survive and succeed.
A persistent bleed from my heart through my skin
So the heart is where I shall begin
To repair what has failed for years.
I have survived typhoons and tidal waves countless times
I have crossed uncrossable lines
And disaster has gratefully let me prepare
For the misfortunes fortunate enough to plague me.

An easy task for they have seen stronger
But they will not weaken me a minute longer
Unknown, a formidable enemy clenches his fist
Executing his plans down the list.
The resilient may at first seem meek
The strong at first, weak
But victory hides in the end
A winner wins at the finish of a race
Not the beginning, soon to be erased.
Others are happy just to place
But winners all the same.
A spirit deserving of a name
But no one word could do justice
Call it a spark or flame
They wonder whom to blame.
For these countless, relentless tries—
The sun dies, the wind cries, and the sea subsides.
You will not hold me back, turbulent sea
For my soul will set fire
As the kindling lay before me.
Fuel for my motor
A motivation unseen by woe or worry
A whirlwind of fury—
Let it strike down
Those who dare subjugate me
Under an umbrella of expectations
That even God would fall short.
But I will not, I refuse
To let abuse abuse me
I remain untouched and will forever be.

THIS WAS THE FIRST POEM I EVER HAD PUBLISHED IN 2004, TWO YEARS BEFORE I WAS diagnosed with bipolar disorder. I remember that this was an assignment for one of my poetry classes at the University of Dayton. This is one of my most polished poems, for it was edited several times before publication. I remember that when I wrote this poem, I felt like there was so much chaos in my life—attending college full-time, and working full-time. I also had a live-in girlfriend, and I was constantly drinking alcohol and smoking marijuana. I was barely sleeping. I did this for almost three years straight. I believe that this chaos was a catalyst in making me ill, but no one really knows.

2 FIRST BREAK

It was like lightning
Struck my brain in two
A feeling I hope never happens to you.
Fueled by a combination
Of drugs and chemical failure
I never even saw it coming.
But in hindsight, they say things seem clearer
The teamwork of genetics, environment, and behavior.
A complete mental meltdown
Of someone competent and capable before
Never having a clue of what tests were in store.
I thought I would get better soon
Not months, into years and more.
Confused, never in control
As the toxic cocktail took its toll
Crammed in a cell and then a bus to court
With total strangers, not knowing what I'd done
Or where I was
But knowing it wasn't normal or fun.
They had me sign some papers

That I couldn't focus to read
And plunged a needle deep in me
And gave me pills they said I'd need.
They took me to a ward where I was greeted
By shrieking vocal cords
They gave me a room, and a short tour
Life as I knew it, never more.
A condition I guess they thought they could fix
July thirty-first, two-thousand and six.

July 31, 2006

THIS IS THE DAY THAT I WAS RUSHED TO THE HOSPITAL, AND THEN DIAGNOSED WITH bipolar disorder with psychotic features. I had to stay in the psychiatric unit for eleven days. I would have to be hospitalized a few times after this too. I haven't been hospitalized since 2012. On that occasion, it was for mania and anxiety/panic. The doctors called it my "first break", which basically means the symptoms of bipolar disorder had become so severe that I was a danger to myself and others and needed to be hospitalized.

3 QUILTED SOFA

Padded checkers and rings
Hold my see-saw feelings
Tragedy, triumph, good, and bad
The best rest I've ever had.
Once glued, now improved
I got back everything
I used to groggily wish for.
Now I seem to be
Trapped in my own clarity.
Truths that will haunt me for years, and fears, dried up tears
Steered by sanity now, but how?
No better time to start than now
Forcing me to stand pat
A curse worse than a black cat
Labels by faces, replaces
All the old thoughts about myself.
But I know who and what I am
Like it or not
Do you really think my soul forgot?

After I was released from the hospital in 2006, I was heavily sedated. I slept on the sofa mentioned in this poem most of the day. All I could manage was to eat and go to the bathroom for the most part.

4 MEDICINAL HAZE

I wake up in a medicinal haze
Left over from the night
And remember all the happy days
And all the ways I used to cope.
Those were times filled with hope.
Now instead of being free,
The doctors pump me full of dope.
With the stroke of his pen
He can control my behavior
Like some holier-than-thou savior.
Saving me from myself
Maybe I did need help
Maybe I'll be better off.
Some people hear disorder
And think it can be cured Like a cold or cough.
But it will never go away, never will
At least the drugs keep me still.
Too still sometimes, more like a zombie
I guess the challenge is
Finding a balance between the new and the old me.

I REMEMBER WRITING THIS POEM ON A REGULAR OLD MORNING. I WAS STILL PRETTY heavily sedated. I was learning to adjust to my "new self", i.e. how the drugs had changed me.

5 JUST A PARK

The sycamore and oak trees
Bow and wave to greet me
And immediately their presence
Makes me feel at peace.
One of my sanctuaries
I've been visiting for years
Not one tall building or store around
Just the trees and me
The rustling of leaves,
the only sound.
Just a quiet spot to simply think
That's all I was really after
No music, conversation, or laughter.
No one to judge me by my fame or wealth
Or to criticize and scrutinize my health
Fields and woody statues
As far as I can see
At this place, in this time,
I can't think of a place I'd rather be.

WHEN I STARTED TO BECOME A LITTLE MORE ALERT, I USED TO DRIVE TO THIS PARK about ten minutes from my house. I would just read a book or write poetry or just sit peacefully and be one with nature. I remember feeling very at peace there. It was near a place called Camp Dennison, near a town called Indian Hill. I haven't been back in years. I need to find time to visit again.

6 POSER FRIENDS

Self-reflection has revealed
An ejection of delusions and false hope.
A more quiet way to cope
Than screaming what I really think of you.
You are the weaker link of a chain now broken
Not even a sentimental token am I left with
A revelation freed from a dark hole
Like a mole, poking its head out for air
Far away in some hand-me-down chair.
If you only knew what you lost
But that's just my perception
No better than the rest, no exception
You are no better friend than I am to you
Never have been
I'd like to cram, all your lies back in your mouth
One by one, 'til you choke
Our "friendship" was just a horrible, cruel joke.
Thanks, once again, poser friend
Your memory will never make me laugh again
I must have run out of what you wanted

Or you would still be around.
All I can say, and I hope you take with you
As penance for all your faults
Locked down tight in mental vaults
I could delicately unravel
But I would rather see you crack and explode.
Blow the doors off, and the landing won't be soft, no loft
Smack against a wall
I could watch you fall over and over again
I saw the end from afar
And now I'm glad to see who you really are.
You piece of nothing, trash on the street
Rancid and sour
And in your final hours, you can explore
The dark abysses you created
And I'm elated to see you doing so poorly.
I used to be concerned surely
When you were someone else...

I WAS ANGRY AT SOME OF MY "POSER FRIENDS" THAT HAD LEFT MY SIDE WHEN I really needed them. The type of people who claimed to be my friends, but then left my side when I was sick.

7 THERE IS HOPE

I lose my mind from time to time
But I always seem to find it
I sometimes get excited about the future
But my past looms right behind it.
Pain that pity and recovery can't resolve
An assortment of memories involved
And plans that never blossomed.
But if anyone thinks for one second
I will give up my hopes and dreams
Just to spite the daily screams.
There's just some things I can't repress
I try to give my all and nothing less.

When I started to come out of "the fog" of the sedatives, I was feeling hopeful because my life was starting to come back together again. I want everyone to know that there is life beyond mental illness, and that "there is hope".

8 STANDING TALL

My head is pounding
And my mind won't quit
The hospital and medications
All because of it.
The sirens scream
Getting closer and closer
Until they are clear as can be.
You can imagine my terror
When I knew they were coming for me.
Laid out on a stretcher
Gasping for air
I wanted to be anywhere but there.
Every second felt like ages
And not a thousand pages
Could capture
How it has come to this.
Never a day goes by
When I don't obsess about it all
But through every single battle
At least I've stood tall.

I've had thousands of panic attacks. This is how I felt during and after. I remember hearing the sirens of the ambulance. I remember not being able to think clearly. At the end of this poem, I'm trying to make myself feel better by thinking and feeling, "At least I've stood tall", and that I have put up a fight.

9 CAME FROM A LONG WAY

When I feel down,
I go back to that place.
The needles and doctors
My mind can't erase.
My concerned friends and family
Who came to visit,
And how my entire life
Is wrapped up in it.
It's everything to me.
It's what drives me to be
A good person and friend.
A success story.
I was down on the mat,
But I got up.
I don't know how or why.
I could have easily given up
And kissed my future goodbye.
I must not be done yet
Or else it would have ended.
My dreams aren't gone,

They just got suspended.
I gave it everything I had
I reached down deep
The memories still haunt me
Even in sleep.
When I have a bad day,
It can always be worse
The curse of making it through.
I give it all I've got
In everything I do.

This is describing my Post Traumatic Stress Disorder that I have from being in the hospital several times, with a touch of hope at the end. My PTSD results in flashbacks and nightmares. I have severe anxiety when I am confronted with anything medically related, or anything that resembles the experiences I've had in hospitals.

10 MONSTER OF PAIN

Behind the laughter and the smiles
There is pain for miles
I've cried so many times
Pleading it will stop.
It always seems to
When it wants to.
Most people don't know what makes me tick.
I don't even know if I do.
Maybe some day I will find out
How and why I got sick.
Maybe because I used to take life for granted
I never appreciated the little things
I just went about going through the motions
Never noticing anything surrounding the path I was on.
Most people have never seen me cry
I hide my emotions well
Every day is as big as a mountain
But you will probably not be able to tell.
My life's an open book
For everyone to read

I like it that way
Nothing to hide
Everything to explain
Like why sometimes
I prefer the rain.
Or why I value the company of friends so much
Or how my thoughts got out of touch.

AROUND 2011-2012, I STARTED ADVOCATING FOR MENTAL ILLNESS AND TELLING MY story. This poem touches on that a bit. When I finally started to "snap out of it", I decided I wanted to be an advocate. I still am to this day, in 2017. I talk about basically putting on a tough front so others don't seem to notice that I am struggling. I wonder what makes me tick, and I wonder if my mental illness is somehow a punishment because I took life for granted when I was younger.

11 BRAIN ON FIRE

My brain is on fire and my mind won't quit
Sometimes, I get sick of all of it.
I fight and I fight, but sometimes it's not enough
I just want to be known as tough.
I have a sense of humor to keep it light
I just want to do what's right.
My purpose is to make people smile and laugh
In that, I firmly believe
You can have all the money and all that comes with it.
I just want to leave a legacy of great stories.
That's what I want to achieve.
That others will commit
To their memories and have a lasting impression in their hearts.
At one time, I was torn apart.
I keep getting up and sometimes I don't know why or how
But I'm a lot closer to knowing now.

THIS POEM IS ABOUT HOW I WANT TO BE REMEMBERED. ONE OF MY LIFE GOALS IS never to be forgotten, or at least not for a very long time. I want to be known as tough and as someone that didn't give up. I want to be that person that makes the best of a bad situation. I talk about finding myself in this battle at the end of the poem. I allude to this battle as being something that has happened for a reason.

12 SMALL TOWN MAN

Right near where the local roads meet the highway,
A man sits and thinks.
He is well-known around his home,
But the small town could not keep him forever.
One day, his name will be heard for miles
And all he can do is smile
Because he knew it would happen all along.
He had dreams about being famous
As long as he could remember
And everything was falling into place.
Not much grace, but there was something special about him.
Intangible, but real.
He could steal hearts in a matter of moments
And he would keep them forever
Because he was loving and loyal.
Far from royal, but he had a distinct strut
Like he had just won at a game.
Many people seem the same,
so he sought out the different to be his friends.
He couldn't care less about trends.

Or money, houses, or cars.
He liked to look up at the stars.
He survived on a little, but it felt like a lot to him.
He knew what it was like to have nothing,
And that feeling always stayed with him.
It helped him be humble and grateful.
Loving, not hateful. Positive, not skeptical.
He never wanted to be a spotlight spectacle.
Just always in others' thoughts
And hopefully those thoughts are fond.
And every time it was needed,
He would answer the bell and respond.

I HAVE A NICE FRONT PORCH ON MY HOUSE THAT I LIKE TO SIT AND THINK AND smoke cigarettes. This poem describes my desire to be somewhat famous, but not valuing material things. I want to be well known, but remain humble. You will definitely keep seeing the theme of me not wanting to be forgotten anytime soon, and to be remembered in a positive light, which really relates to my obsession with death and dying.

13 BEACH

The sun shoots its rays
Across the expansive sky
Reflected off the water like glass
And I start to wonder why.
Anyone would wake to anything else
The clouds hanging over like cream
This is the morning most are forced to dream.
For some, an actuality
But they probably stopped looking
Thinking about bills, or errands for the day
While the sorrowful are longing
For such a sight to behold.
A scene, to some, has turned old.
But if I ever have a chance
To hear the waves crash and see the foam dance
The amazing sun and clouds overhead
I will rush to meet the sea.
But then what would I think about
To keep me restful in my bed?

I live in Cincinnati, Ohio, so I am far from the ocean. This poem is basically just me describing a daydream about the beach and ocean. I describe the daydream, but then wonder if it would be ruined if I actually got to experience my daydream (i.e. "but then what would I think about to keep me restful in my bed?").

14 LET ME GO

If you are done with me, let me go.
I've died several times.
I obsess over death. I dream about it.
I pray for it.
Until that time comes, let me live.
I don't want to be here halfway.
I have a job to do, and we both know it.
I need all the strength and courage I can hold.
I will leave nothing left untold.
My soul was meant to be shared.
It was really never mine.
It wasn't supposed to be like this, but here we are.
I've already come so far.
Don't let me go just yet. I have work to do.
I just need a little relief.
Forgive me for my beliefs, and all I have done wrong.
I want my list of good deeds to be long.
So when we meet, I can stand proud.
So when I sing, I can sing out loud.

The only thing I have ever been sure of is that I wanted to be a good person
And help those in need.
Why must I bleed?

THIS POEM IS ABOUT MY FRUSTRATION WITH STRUGGLING TO DO SMALL TASKS. I AM frustrated, but at the same time, I have "work to do" (advocate for the mentally ill). I am almost pleading to God, or gods, or the Fates, to "let me go, if you are finished with me". This also fits the theme of death that you have seen in other poems.

15 BROKEN DOWN

I feel broken
Usually unspoken.
It's a trembling,
Sometimes it seems unending.
My chest hurts,
In short bursts,
But I've learned it's not alarming.
It's disarming, I'm charming,
When I feel like myself.
And it all figures somehow
But don't ask me how.
I'm dizzy, light-headed
Scary memories, embedded.
I can't shake it, or take it
I just try to survive and make it.
I feel shattered,
I matter,
At least that's what they tell me.
I don't trust my instincts,
Or gut feels

My mind runs like hamster wheels.
It's be nice not to think at all for a while
And when I hit a wall,
I go around it or through it.
It's like I always knew it.

This is basically just how I feel on a regular basis. This alludes to racing thoughts ("my mind races like hamster wheels"), and also mania, where it's hard to trust my own judgment (instincts).

16 LUCKY STARS

As I've gotten older
I carry around the hurt
As a chip on my shoulder.
I carry it around as a fire inside
When it starts burning
There's nowhere to hide.
I carry it around
As a weight on my back
Sometimes I can't shake it
Sometimes I look back.
I carry it around
Like concrete in my shoes
Hard to move forward
But refusing to lose.
Making giant steps
Stumble by stumble
Sometimes it's too much
But it keeps me humble.
A mind that doesn't stop
Cranking and cranking

It keeps me occupied
And it keeps me thanking
My lucky stars
For what could have been.
How it could be.
I focus more on that
Than how it should be.

This poem is about having a positive attitude, and never giving up. I allude to focusing on how it is and how it should be. I don't think it's therapeutic to think of the way things should or could be. I don't think it's productive to think life's not fair. I think it's in my best interest to deal with life as it has been given to me.

17 CHILD GIANT

They all knew
He didn't belong
In a chair, anywhere
The desk wouldn't even hold him.
He sat in discomfort
Most of the time
And the teachers would often scold him.
He towered over the children
And more wit than the teachers
He disobeyed most rules
And challenged the preachers.
He was told things he had already been taught
Five years earlier, and never forgot.
A class clown
And a teacher's pet
All the lessons he would never forget.
A kind and gentle giant of a child
Calm and collected, with a touch of wild
Slow to anger
Quick to peace

A hunger for knowledge
Never ceased

This is my perception of how I was when I was a child. Or maybe other people's perception. In a way, it is arrogant to think I didn't belong "in a chair, anywhere" (i.e. a desk as in school). People with bipolar disorder often think highly of themselves. Also called grandiose feelings.

18 MY DARKEST HOUR

And in my darkest hour
You had a kind word
My brain wasn't working
But I somehow still heard.
I remember your smiles
When my memory was lost
I remember the visits
At such a cost.
I remember your concern
At every single step
I remember how sad you were
Even while I slept.
I'll never forget
When you gave me your heart
Even when our souls
Were miles apart.
Even then
I still never forgot
All the love you gave
Towards the story, and the plot

I'm here today
Doing pretty well
Mostly because of you
And partly from going through hell.
There will still be those that don't believe
Everything I say
I've had some awful moments
And I still count the days.
I've learned a great deal
About life and about myself
I've taken all your acts
And placed them on a shelf
Any given moment I can reach back in time
And remember what you gave me
Truly sublime.

THIS POEM IS ABOUT ALL THE SUPPORT I HAVE RECEIVED SINCE 2006 FROM FAMILY and friends. It's worth mentioning that some people with mental illness have little to no support.

19 WONDERING ABOUT EVERYTHING

Many times a day I wonder
How many nights I have left
I wonder if I would even want to know.
I wonder if I am living right
When the world tells me 'no'.
I wonder if Fate will smile kindly on me
And let me be around.
I wonder if I have done enough work
Before they lay me in the ground.
Or let the wind take my ashes to the sea
That's really the only place I wish to be.
I try to imagine how far the stars are away
And if I will get to see one up-close some day.
I only know how to live one way—
The simplest way I possibly can.
And at the same time
Leaving the Earth a good man.

HERE IS THE THEME OF NOT BEING FORGOTTEN EASILY AGAIN. I OFTEN THINK ABOUT death. It's listed as one of the symptoms of bipolar disorder. Death or dying is a theme that you will see.

20 DEATH STARE

Only when you've stared death in the face
And survive
Only then are you truly alive.
Live like it is your last day
Don't make it something you just say.
I know this from experience
It's not some theoretical idea to me
I consider it a blessing to be
Reminded so soon of my mortality.
Some sail through life, no worries, and that's great
But this is not a lesson you want to learn late.
Let me be an example
And lend your ear
The struggles I have had, I hope you are never near.
And to you, I say good luck
Painting the canvas of life
And I hope your days are filled
With not a bit of strife.
But if life deals you an altering hitch
I can only wish

You find the strength to carry on
May all your troubles be short, and your days be long.

THIS IS ME TRYING TO BE POSITIVE AFTER A PANIC ATTACK. I TRULY WISH THE BEST for everyone. That is another theme you might see. I have a lot of love in my heart, despite everything.

21 WHILE IN SLEEP

Words that are jumbled
Explosions of neon greens...
And brilliant bursts of blue.
A nervous, unsettling, spasm of moves.
Sleep comes in spurts
But it's never enough.
Dreams hardly come
And nightmares are plenty.
Wide awake and sweating.
The damage has been done.
If only memories had filters
And we could pick and choose
The ones to forget, and the ones we don't want to lose.
Work with what you're given,
As hard as that may be
You may find it will suffice.
Always know your worth
But never tag yourself a price.

I WROTE THIS POEM AFTER A BAD NIGHT'S SLEEP. I TRY TO BE ENCOURAGING AS well. There is another theme. Sometimes when I close my eyes, I see colors that I can only describe as pink and blue cotton candy, and they burst and dance like some kind of visual effects show.

22 THE GRAVEYARD DANCERS

If life's so easy
And not so hard
Why do I believe
They are dancing in the graveyard?
Laughing when we drive past
With convincing looks it will all last
Stress and and blur our thoughts
At least the dead are never lost
And never feel the need for greed
No violence or destruction
Not to ever have to bleed
Or the pressure to succeed.
If you deem these thoughts bizarre
Try looking out from the graveyard.

Here is the theme of death and dying again. I wrote about wondering if the dead have any pain or problems. I also wonder if I would be better off dead because at least I wouldn't be suffering.

23 THE WINDS OF LOVE

His heart settled for a draw,
But it felt more like a loss.
He tried to adjust his sails,
But the winds of love
Would just blow across.
He could only do things halfway
Because he never felt complete.
He found solace in solitude,
And the material world could not compete.
He surrounded himself in knowledge,
And learned and taught many things.
But he could never find, in any book,
The joy that love brings.

This is about the heartbreak of not being able to find love in a mate. I also don't value material things too much anymore. I love learning, and I'm still unsure whether solitude is what I want.

24 MAN ON A MISSION

I hope Heaven and Hell can wait.
I hope I arrive surrounded by love and late.
It's not my decision,
I'm just a man on a mission.
My life is in the hands of Fate.
I hope Heaven and Hell can wait.

This is another poem about my mortality. I feel like my "mission" is to be a mental health advocate and spread the word about mental illness.

25 SOAR INTO THE HEAVENS

I hope I soar into the heavens
Far above the sky.
I know I'll see all the angels
That too early, passed us by.
I want to meet all the saints
And ask them a lot of questions
Maybe over a nice dinner
And talk about the people I want to mention.
Maybe it will be an ocean
And I'll fall into the darkest depths
A peaceful place of silence
Filled with tears we all wept.
But maybe I'll be sent to Hell
The fire and smoky air—
A place for only a few
But I think I've already been there.

Here is the theme of death again and me wondering about the afterlife. Also describing the "Hell" that I have been through.

26 A STURDY HOUSE

I built a house made of paper,
But it all came crashing down.
It all came crashing down.
I drove a car as far as I could drive,
But I wrecked along the way.
I wrecked along the way.
I took a bus to the end of the line,
But it went spinning of the road.
Spinning off the road.
I took a plane to the edge of the world,
But it fell before I got there.
It fell before I got there.
I built a boat that could stand a mighty wind,
But it sank to the bottom.
It sank to the bottom.
I built a life made of promises and hope,
But it all came crashing down.
It all came crashing down.
And then I stopped building,

And I just started creating things.
And nothing could bring them down.
Nothing could bring them down.

This is a celebration of the creative arts, and the denouncement of material things.

27 IF IT'S THE LAST THING I DO

If it's the last thing I do,
Let it be kind,
So I can have a clear mind.
If it's the last thing I do,
Let it be courageous
Because no one respects a coward.
If it's the last thing I do,
Let it be out of love
Because I want to leave it all for you,
And I have so much to give.
If it's the last thing I do,
Let it be noble
Because I want to leave proud.
If it's the last thing I do,
Let it show my strength
Because I have the heart of a lion.
If it's the last thing I do,
Let it be thoughtful
Because my intentions are good.
If it's the last thing I do,

Let it be creative
Because I have so much to share.
If it's the last I do,
Let it show character.
And if it's the last thing I do,
Let it be memorable.

COMMON THEMES OF DEATH AND BEING REMEMBERED ARE REPEATED AGAIN HERE. Also my unwillingness to quit.

28 THE TERROR OF PANIC

In that place
All I feel is fear
And thoughts about death Are near.
When it is through,
I just want to cry.
Another step backwards
Telling myself all I can do is try.
Enough to bring a big man
To his knees
And pray for it to be over
Begging for the end, please!
A terror so potent
Minutes feel like days
Feelings so strong
My ego always pays.
I never know when it will come
I just know I'm grateful when it's done
I sometimes wish I were the only one.
I just want someone to tell me it's okay
I just want the words to help convey

How awful the panic really can be
If you could only see
How crippling it really is
How painful and strong.
Not matter how short, it always seems long.
And I always feel wronged.
What did I do?
I try to be a good person
And do what's right
I try and work hard
And I'm thankful at night.
I know deep down it's not my fault
But I always retrace my actions
And my past deeds
Even though I know I can't go back
I think if I do enough good
I can cover my tracks.
But the fact is,
Nothing I did
Has anything to do with me now
For some reason, I have been chosen
To make lemonade somehow.
I don't want your pity
That's not the point
I can't say enough
To get anyone to feel how terrible it can be
I wouldn't wish it on my worst enemy.

My description and feelings about a panic attack.

29 LIFE CREEPS UP

We all want perfect little lives,
With everything in a row,
But that's rarely how it goes.
Life creeps up, and life creeps in,
And it forces us to change plans.
Some things are best unplanned,
While others seem too much to bear.
We are left gasping for air,
But soon it all passes.
And we start to pick up the pieces,
Pretending nothing ever happened.
But then, life creeps up, and life creeps in,
Forcing us to change the plans again.

THIS POEM IS ABOUT HOW LIFE CAN BE VERY UNORGANIZED, AS MUCH AS WE WANT everything planned out.

30 NOT A TIME FOR SYMPATHY

I don't need your sympathy.
I'll make some coffee
And have a cup with me.
Our roads crossed for some reason
Time don't matter or the season
But I don't need your sympathy.
We can talk until our tongues go dry
And if we need to
We can wipe each other's eyes.
I just love your company
But I don't need your sympathy.
I'll light a smoke while you're talking
And I'll listen the best I can
I want to hear your point of view
And all the things that make up you
But I don't need your sympathy.
I don't have close to all the answers
But maybe we have some common ground.
I just want to make you feel better
I know pain and I know healing

But I don't need your sympathy.
Our talk is over now and it's time to go
Maybe we can do this again
If I say I am your friend,
I will be one to the end,
But I don't need your sympathy.

THIS POEM IS ABOUT HOW I DON'T WANT PEOPLE TO FEEL SORRY FOR ME, AND HOW I am almost always available to listen to a friend's problems. Also, that I enjoy just sitting and talking about life and whatever else. On a lighter note, I really enjoy coffee and smoking cigarettes on my front porch.

31 PSYCH WARD

Nightmares from the psych ward....
Nightmares from the psych ward....
Flashed back to the day
When I was locked away
They all tell me
That it was the only way.
Meet your new master, the Queen of Disaster,
She's going to let you know how it goes.
I had to behave, so that I could have a shave
I was lucky to even remember my name.
Every single day, trying to find a way to get out
And I wondered what this was all about.
Every so often, I would hear a shout
Either staff or the committed.
They said I belonged there,
But I refused to admit it.
I still don't know what they dosed me with,
But I took a long, deep sleep.
I woke up so foggy that they knew they could keep me.

Nice and calm now, here's a bunch of questions.
We'll let you know when we think you're alright.

This poem describes nightmares and flashbacks to when I was hospitalized in the psychiatric unit in 2006.

32 FINALLY ON TOP

He was broken down,
Stepped on,
And will be buried in the ground.
But the demons will not go with him.
His soul shined bright as a star
Reflected through a diamond prism.
While alive, he kept marching,
And after every single fall, he got up.
He would not quit and refused to lose.
A battle he didn't get to choose.
A peaceful man, with a warrior's fight
Even though he didn't sleep at night.
The shadows danced wherever he looked,
But he just learned to ignore them.
The voices never stopped either,
But again, he lived through it.
Even he didn't understand why he kept getting up.
Maybe he wanted to be a legend.
Maybe when he's finally at rest,
He wants to be remembered as a man that never gave up.

Maybe he wants to be an inspiration and example
To everyone that is facing hard times.
Although he didn't always understand,
He understood never to stop.
And when it's all said and done,
With any luck,
He will finally end up on top.

THIS FITS THE THEME ABOUT DEATH AND BEING REMEMBERED AGAIN. I WAS thinking that when my life is over, I can finally rest and "end up on top". I hope I have left a positive imprint on the world. To me, that's what it means to "end up on top".

33 STANDING MY GROUND

I will not lay down my sword in defeat.
I will die with it in my hand.
I will not retreat.
You can kill me where I stand.
I've already faced the worst,
So nothing really scares me.
I have nothing to lose,
So all your threats, you can spare me.
I don't back down. I don't quit.
Yes, sometimes I get sick of all of it. I will admit.
But fear and me got to be friends through the years.
So you can speak your negative talk into someone else's ears.

THIS POEM IS ABOUT STAYING POSITIVE IN THE FACE OF ADVERSITY AND NOT giving up.

34 YOU CAN'T TAKE EVERYTHING

The tears sting sweetly
As they roll down my face.
And things were taken from me
That can't be replaced.
But I'm not bitter or angry or sad.
I can't go on that feeling that way.
But it's still hard to believe
All the words that you say.
Like you love me and you are proud.
Down deep, I know them to be true.
But when I hear them out loud,
There's only so much healing they can do.

I WROTE THIS POEM AFTER I HAD BEEN CRYING. IT SPEAKS TO HOW I FEEL THAT I AM damaged and broken, no matter how much everyone encourages me.

35 THE END

As I watched clouds explode
And stars collide
The sky swallowed itself in submission.
An event for no one's eyes—
But that night
With my mind's permission
I witnessed the grim possibility of the future.
The catastrophic, violent images
Disturbed me enough to retreat
And run from the Creator and Destroyer
No hope for success, the inevitable demise
But that's not what our state implies
And when greed, power, and money combine
They will leave nothing behind.
As soon as I woke
I pleaded to the silence
To never let me see the day
When the sunshine goes away.

THIS IS ABOUT A DREAM I HAD ABOUT THE END OF THE WORLD.

36 MY RESTING MIND

Usually when my mind is racing
I write my best
But today my mind is taking a rest.
Not thinking much at all
Unusual for me.
A sense of peace and calm
Bathed in mirth and security.
My thoughts are not frantic
Unusual for me.
Feeling pretty fantastic
But never to the highest degree.
Not too sluggish
Or nerves standing on end.
No negative thinking
And realizing I just bend
Never break.
If I could only find which road to take.

THIS IS DESCRIBING MY USUAL SYMPTOMS AND HOW THEY ARE ABSENT WHILE I WAS writing this. It also alludes to not really having a set direction and general uncertainty with my life.

37 PAINT YOU A PICTURE

I tried to paint you a picture.
I'm not much of an artist, but I can get by.
I don't have many secrets left,
Or too many lies.
I told you my feelings that I kept inside.
It seems like so long now.
I wonder who noticed. I wonder who read.
I wonder who chose to ignore it all instead.
I do what I can with what I have.
And I'm giving it all I can.
The words had to come out,
From my head straight out my hands.
I don't ask for much, because I really don't need it
I can do without a lot.
I prefer it that way actually,
Life can make you ill, the more that is sought.
I do better with less. Less mess. Less hassle.
Less stress. Less worry.
But it's still all a little blurry.
I'm feeling my way through

To fight another day.
I wonder if it will all ever go away.

This poem is about how I tried to "paint a picture" of what mental illness looks like in my first book. One last theme that you have seen throughout this book is that I keep fighting and don't give up.

38 MY LASTING WISH

Most of all I wish you joy
Happiness beyond measure
Infinite pleasure
And satisfaction with your life.
Only you are you
And it is who you were meant to be
Don't wish to be someone else
You were made perfectly.
If you should fall, pick yourself up
And I wish for you, an overflowing cup.
Try to be kind and increasingly wise
There isn't much else
As much as I can surmise.
I want for you the very best
And I mean that more than you know
I hope you find a blissful place
A respite, in your mind, you can go.
Don't spend too much time
On sadness and despair
Seconds are precious

And there are no flowers there.
Pick up the pieces, one by one
Until you feel whole
Nothing will ever be perfect
Not everything you can control.
Try to be your best
Every single day
Show the world your greatness
In every single way.

I WANTED TO END THE BOOK WITH THIS POEM. I TRULY, FROM THE BOTTOM OF MY heart, wish everyone the best. Friend or foe. I have no hostility towards anyone. I want every person to be the best that they can be and to try their best. Love and best wishes, always....

John Medl
THE LAST
DAY OF
JULY
13 Years of Madness

INTRODUCTION

This book is a collection of journal entries about my life and symptoms along with letters to various people and organizations. Many of the journal entries are out of order, but I will do my best to explain each entry. My entire purpose of being an author and mental health advocate is to help people not feel so alone, and also to inspire others with my life story. Mental illness is a constant struggle, and often times, just getting through the day is a victory. I've tried to set the standards for my life at a higher level, but I am also struggling along with a lot of my readers too. My writings are not just for the ill, but their friends and family as well to help understand what someone who has a mental disorder may go through in a day, week, or years.

1 SENIOR REFLECTION PAPER

John Medl
Senior Reflection Paper
English 4 CP1

THE KEYSTONE READS 1959. I APPROACH THE LUMINOUS STRUCTURE, MY COLLARED shirt and khaki shorts drenched in sweat on a hot late-August day. I am a freshman attending Archbishop Moeller High School for the first day in my high school career. The walls loom over my head as if to mock me, complemented by brass figurines perched on top of championship pedestals. All around are strange faces, except the dozen or so children that I had known since I was in first grade. I planned to sneak into Moeller without talking to too many people, get good grades, a diploma, go to college, and have Moeller not bat an eye at my existence. Familiarity and popularity were very familiar to me as a smaller child. I excelled in knothole sports (biggest kid on the team and probably the best). I've lived in the same house all my life in a small town, and I was somewhat of a troublemaker. All those combined with myself being a nice kid, funny for my age, and I could not walk two blocks in Deer Park without recognition. I wanted to stay away from that, not because I didn't like it, but simply because I knew the feeling. I wanted to be different at Moeller, just for the adventure and unpredictability of different. I would talk to my old friends who knew me already, stay in my corner of the school, and just get out. I realize how immature this train of thought was, but I believe I was very immature when I entered Moeller. I thought smart people got good grades, and bad people were the ones in jail. I thought that was how the world worked when I entered high school.

As I proceeded through my education at Moeller, I maintained decent grades, but learned more important lessons in the process. I learned that everyone is so different, and no one can be generalized. I learned that when I treat others how I want to be treated, it might work or not, but I did my part. Those who responded positively I began to pursue relationships with, and those who responded negatively, I did not. I knew they wanted to be nice, but there was something about them I probably didn't understand. I also realized that people are not always the person I see every day, but may be hiding behind something. I've struggled to realize if that is my job, to try and help those people, or simply let them figure it out like I did. I began to develop pretty close friends that I had not known three years earlier. I was amazed at the concept of a new friendship. It had been so long for me to remember what a NEW friendship was like. I started to see the majority of the class as individuals instead of the people I didn't go to grade school with. I really started to enjoy my participation at Moeller. The epitome of when I felt the most unified in my class at Moeller was the state basketball game in Columbus versus Shaker Heights, a team heavily favored to win. The emotions, the unity, the excitement of winning our first state basketball title made me feel like I was almost the one who received the alley-oop pass to slam the game-clincher home. I felt I was out there along with the entire student body. I will never forget that.

Looking back, I will always remember that I am not always right and I should listen to everyone's opinion in search for the best result. Maturity is the acceptance of your faults, I believe, and then dealing with these faults. I will always remember how it feels to be made fun of, excluded, so that I may be able to help those who feel excluded. I have used those instances only to make me stronger. I know that not necessarily all overachievers have it together, and have problems just like underachievers. I like that the main thing I have learned about life while at Moeller can be summed up in three sentences: All people are unique and have distinct personalities, but all deserving of equal respect. Do not judge other lest you be judged. Treat your neighbor as yourself.

I never thought Bible quotes would ever be applicable to my own life, but I realize that I was being close-minded to familiarity again. It's funny most people want to be known or popular, but I wanted to be common. I eventually broke out of that idea and became a pretty well-known figure on campus. I will take all that I have learned at Moeller and use it to help me succeed, and the hallowed hallways of Moeller have produced another man, John Medl.

2 1N5.ORG

This is a letter I wrote to the Cincinnati-based non-profit organization, 1N5.org. Their mission is to stop the stigma surrounding mental illness through advocacy. They have fundraisers and share stories of people who are fighting the battle of mental illness. They have a website and can also be found all across social media.

To Whom It May Concern,

I hope that sharing my story helps others within your organization. I was first diagnosed with bipolar disorder with psychotic features in 2006. Since then, I have been diagnosed with panic disorder/generalized anxiety disorder, posttraumatic stress disorder, obsessive-compulsive disorder, agoraphobia, and claustrophobia. I have dedicated my life to helping others, spreading awareness, and ending stigma. I have a social media page, for which I am the administrator named "Mental Health Awareness and Online Support". I am also a published poet at maverickmagazine.com. Both are free resources for anyone interested. I have written 3 books, with my newest book just published titled, "The Last Day of July: 13 Years of Madness". All 3 books are available online. Thanks for your time in reading my story.

Sincerely,
John E. Medl

3 38TH BIRTHDAY

This next entry was when I was reflecting on my life on my 38th birthday in October of 2019.

38 THINGS I'VE LEARNED IN THE LAST 38 YEARS:

1. Love is the most powerful force on Earth
2. Most things we worry about don't matter
3. Kindness is never the wrong thing to do
4. You don't have to be rich to be charitable and generous
5. Broad social change starts with an individual. (Thanks, Prof. Connelly)
6. Every day has the potential to be a good day
7. A loving family and good friends are priceless
8. The world is full of good people. If you can't find one, be one.
9. People who put you down don't like something about themselves
10. The world is changed by your example, not your opinion
11. Apologize whenever necessary
12. Everyone runs this race we call life at all different paces
13. Money can be a great thing, but don't let it run your life

14. Being positive and having a grateful heart really helps in tough situations
15. The world is full of suffering, but it is also full of people overcoming it
16. Recovery from tragedy is not linear
17. Perfection is not an option
18. There are many varieties of intelligence
19. If you tell the truth, you don't have to remember anything
20. Even the smartest person on the planet only knows a small amount of all there is to know
21. Dream big
22. Don't let mistakes define you
23. You don't get an award for being right. Sometimes, it's worth it to walk away from arguments.
24. Forgiveness is an attribute of the strong.
25. Sometimes a kick in the teeth is what you need at the time
26. Never give up; there is dignity in fighting
27. Integrity is doing the right thing even when no one is looking
28. Fix the cause. Not just the symptoms.
29. Practice your craft. You will statistically get better.
30. A career is a job. A vocation is a calling.
31. The thing people will remember most about you is how you treated them.
32. It is not any of our jobs to judge others
33. Everyone you meet is fighting a battle you know nothing about
34. You meet everyone for a reason
35. Not everyone you lose is a loss
36. Eat, drink, and be merry
37. Prayer never hurts
38. You only get so many birthdays

4 HOME BOUND SENIOR CITIZENS

THIS NEXT ENTRY IS A LETTER I WROTE TO HOME BOUND SENIOR CITIZENS FOR Christmas.

Hello, I hope this card brightens your day and your holidays! My name is John, and I attended St. Saviour school for all 8 years, and then Moeller High School and The University of Dayton. I wanted to send you a Christmas card to let you know that there are so many people that care about you and are praying for you this Christmas season. I'm hoping for a white Christmas, but I don't have to travel. I hope you have plenty of loved ones to share the season with, and if you don't, this card is a reminder that people care about you, even people you have never met before. MERRY CHRISTMAS!

5 COMMISSIONER OF MAJOR LEAGUE BASEBALL

I WAS GIVEN A SIGNED BASEBALL BY THE COMMISSIONER OF MAJOR LEAGUE Baseball after I wrote him this letter.

Dear Commissioner Manfred,

I would like to request an autographed baseball from you. I'm not exactly sure if that is how it works. It seems very generous of you. I collect Cincinnati sports memorabilia, so that's why I am interested in an autographed baseball. I will include my address at the end of this letter. If you can't oblige, that's okay. I will just tell you a few of my thoughts about baseball. I was lucky to play on a little league team for ten years when I was a child. I am thirty-three years old now. Those were the best times of my life. My dad and I watch every Cincinnati Reds game that is available on TV/Cable. It's one of the only things we have always had in common.

I really like what you have done for the speed of the game. The games go much quicker, but not too fast. I know people get touchy when you start talking about changing in general, but the rules of baseball more so. I think you are doing a fantastic job with suspensions and penalties as well. Criminals, PEDs, and any form of cheating belittles the integrity of the game and should not be tolerated.

I would not be a good Reds fan (for my whole life) unless I give a mention to Pete Rose being allowed to be on the ballot for the Hall of Fame. I know you know that many players, former and current, have done much worse. I think the man has done his time for his crimes against baseball. Regardless, he is the greatest hitter of all time. No one can take that away from him. It would be nice if he took his rightful spot in the Hall with all the other greats.

There is a topic that is near and dear to my heart that I need to mention too. That's mental illness. I was diagnosed with bipolar disorder in 2006, and since then, Obsessive Compulsive Disorder, Panic Disorder, Generalized Anxiety Disorder, and agoraphobia have been added to my complete diagnosis. I have not seen a night in baseball in any stadium devoted to mental illness, and to the people who are suffering and the ones we have lost to suicide. I know it is not a happy topic, but it would be great if MLB could do something for one night in every stadium. A lime green ribbon is our symbol. The statistics are staggering for how common mental illness is. I believe that as many as one in three people have some type of mental illness. I volunteer my time every day to a social media page that I created for mental illness awareness. I am also a published author of my life story titled, "Millions Like Me: My Struggle with Mental Illness". I am a published poet at maverickmagazine.com as well. Thank you so much for your time and devotion to the betterment of the game.

Sincerely,
John E. Medl

6 MUNCHIES

Many years ago, I hit a parked car going about 10mph. Nothing bad happened, but they took me by ambulance to the hospital to get checked out. I had about two beers and I took a hit or two off a joint. They did a blood test to check for drugs, and nothing significant showed up.

I was sitting there with two African-American police officers, and I kinda had the munchies, and I said, "Do you have anything to eat around here?"

One of the cops said, "We might have some juice or crackers."

So I said, "What did you call me?" We all had a good laugh.

7 THE DOCTOR

I HAVE TO SEE THE DOCTOR TODAY, WHICH IS USUALLY UNPLEASANT, BUT I FEEL pretty good today. I've been upset about this appointment for weeks. Luckily, I was able to still enjoy the holidays the best I could, although I'm not much of a festive person. I'm lucky that I have a doctor I like, and we are on a first name basis. He reminds me of a "bro"....maybe someone I would be friends with outside of the clinical setting. He is very proud of me, and he's very easygoing and easy to talk to.

I have some good news to tell him today, but I also have a lot of questions about my progress. I am getting to the point where my anxiety when leaving the house is too much to bear, and I have extreme irritability on a fairly regular basis. I don't know how much I can expect from my brain and body, which really is the whole mystery about mental illness. It's a lot of trial and error, whether it be medication or cognitive therapy.

There's no road map, and there's no magic pill. Some of the work has to be done by the patient (me). Right now, I have high anxiety when leaving the house and low energy, almost always. I want to see if that can be improved, either with a medicine change or other cognitive therapy. One thing is for sure: I have fought the whole time. It's one of my redeeming qualities. I hope when my life is over that being a fighter is one of the main things people remember about me, followed by how much I loved and gave to others.

8 DOCTOR BEN

I HAVEN'T DONE MUCH JOURNALING SINCE I FINISHED MY LAST BOOK IN JULY 2019, which has been a nice break, but I wanted to share a few things today about my progress and mental illness in general. I have to see my doctor today, who simply wants me to call him Ben. Really awesome, younger guy. Very smart, kind, and approachable. I really like him as my doctor. It's going to be a great feeling when I hand him a copy of my new book. He was very impressed that I had written so much the last time I saw him. It seemed like he was just generally impressed by the work I do, and my insight into my illness.

I'm glad the day of my appointment is finally here, so I know that it will all be over by this afternoon. I'm in better shape, anxiety-wise than usual, and overall, it is getting easier to see the doctor now that I am on a 3 month schedule rather than every month. Within the last few years, I used to have major anxiety and panic attacks at the doctor. My chest hurt and my head felt foggy every time I saw the doctor. I used to have to steady myself against the wall sometimes just to keep my balance.

One thing I want to say about mental illness is that there's no real clear cut objectives. No finish line or deadlines for improvement. Yes, things like taking a shower, driving, and socializing have gotten easier for me, and I guess that's because I kept trying. When I drove myself downtown the other day, that was a major accomplishment, but there's no guarantee that I can do it today or tomorrow. It's all so subjective and case-by-case. I know people with bipolar disorder that have full-time careers. That is not possible for me right now. If I was in proper shape, mentally and physically, I would try to apply for a career other than writing. It's just frustrating that there's no end game. Am I a success now? I would say yes. Is it possible that I could return to work eventually? Probably, but again, there's no guarantees. Just wanted to share my thoughts for a minute.

9 PROGRESS

When I saw the doctor yesterday, I was totally ready to change my medications, as scary as that idea sounded. I talked to my doctor, and he was actually happy with my progress. He told me he took the time to read through my medical records (over 13 years' worth) and my books, and I really have come a long way. Like almost miraculous.

I feel pretty good most of the time. It's at least tolerable. I don't expect to feel perfect all the time. I told him a lot of feelings and thoughts I have, and he basically pointed out that I overthink a lot of things, which I kinda already knew.

He told me I have to find ways to turn my brain off, per se. Music, crossword puzzles, whatever works. Writing about all of this really helps me, and I know it helps others as well. Another part of shutting down my brain is taking time for myself to recharge my batteries before I do too much advocating. Everything I do doesn't have to be for a cause or to help others.

The doctor was more concerned with my mood being stable and that I was getting enough sleep. He wasn't even concerned that I gained 12 pounds, but I am. I have to work on that. I'm still down 38 pounds overall, however, so I'm not starting from scratch. My BP was 138/88, which I have no idea what that means, but I know it's always high at the doctor's office. My pulse is always elevated too.

I had a brief panic attack when I got in my mom's van to go to the appointment, but I got out, and took some deep breaths, and I was able to keep the appointment. I'm really glad it's over until almost April. I found that riding in the back seat helps, for whatever reason. Maybe because I'm not right up on the dash or something.

He recommended therapy (CBT) for my cognition, but I'm still thinking if I want to make that commitment. It was nice to be reminded that I have made so much progress, but I'm also looking forward to the challenge of improving little things in my life that might make a big difference.

10 ELLEN DEGENERES

THIS IS A LETTER I WROTE TO ELLEN DEGENERES, AND I INCLUDED A COPY OF MY first book. I think this was sometime around 2014.

Hi Ellen! (Ms. DeGeneres is probably more appropriate, but it doesn't feel right. I think of you as such a kind, humble person)

Here is a copy of my book. It's my life story, detailing my struggle with mental illness. I have been diagnosed with bipolar disorder with psychotic features, generalized anxiety disorder/panic disorder, posttraumatic stress disorder, claustrophobia, and agoraphobia. I would be honored if you just gave it a read. I remember watching your sitcom as a younger adult, and it was hilarious. As I started watching your talk show, I saw again how funny you are, but I also saw such a humble, happy, and kind soul. Thanks for any time you give me.

Love and Best Wishes,
John Edward Medl
johnmedl7@gmail.com

11 QUEEN BEE

I HOPE YOU FIND THIS AS FUNNY AS I DO....THE DYNAMIC OF MY HOUSEHOLD GOES like this—Mom pretty much controls the household and knows everything that's going on. My dad has veto power, but in a limited capacity. I am the low man on the totem pole, and I try to just mind my own business and keep to myself whenever possible. All of us get along fairly well, all things considered, UNTIL the balance of power is messed with. All of this leads me to the day when my dad said something so funny to my mom. My mom was trying to tell my dad what clothes to wear or that he needed a jacket or something, and my dad was just like, "I think I can do what I want". Wrong thing to say to Queen Bee! LOL

12 HOOKAHVILLE

I have been to many Hookahvilles, starting around 1998. Hookahville is a weekend-long music festival where the band Ekoostik Hookah is the main act. My last Hookahville was Spring 2006, or whichever one that was when Blues Traveler was there.

I used to go to all kinds of concerts, but I was diagnosed with bipolar disorder and anxiety, so I don't leave my house much, and large crowds intimidate me. Well, I decided to step outside my comfort zone and go see my friends' band, The Summit, (with Ekoostik Hookah) around November of last year. My buddy, Mike Hennel, (drummer for The Summit), introduced me to Eric, the drummer for Hookah. I told Eric a little about my story and he asked if I had any requests. I honestly couldn't believe Eric was even asking me. When I was growing up, Hookah were some of my heroes. You never really think of ever meeting them or connecting with them on a personal level. The only songs I could think of were Ohio Grown and Loner. Sure enough, right as I was about to leave (early) for the night, Hookah played Loner! I like to believe it was for me :) Much love to you all! (Hookah later confirmed that the song Loner was, in fact, for me). What a great night.

13 PANIC ATTACK

Sometimes, it's our own bullshit that is holding us back. No one tries to trigger me or upset me. It just happens. It's hard to know how much I can actually control how I react. I have to train my mind to not worry and overthink so much, which is quite a battle. I have to work at it.

The worst panic attack I've had in the last couple months was in the beginning of November 2019, and I was tempting the Fates. I drank coffee and didn't allow my medicine to work properly before getting in the car. I knew better. I don't know why I thought I could sneak something like that past my illness that day. Being successful takes extreme care, caution, maintenance, and constant attempts to improve.

14 GETTING CAUGHT UP

I've been foolish lately, or perhaps, just human. I have been getting caught up in the struggle and stress of daily life, and I have been forgetting how blessed I am. I can't believe my life has turned out the way it has. Thank you all to everyone who has supported me in any way. I don't really know anyone with a mental illness who has as much support as I do, not that it's a competition, obviously. I have everything and everyone that I need, but the more good people, the merrier.

15 FEAR

Fear is a part of anxiety, but I wouldn't say I'm always scared when I have anxiety. I bring this up because I need to drive and run some errands today. Not an emergency or anything. My mom will run them for me if I can't do it. I'm lucky in that regard. But driving is so difficult for me because there is definitely a fear present, but I also have physical symptoms like numbness in my arms, dizziness, and chest pains. It's really hard for me to understand because I used to drive for a living. I guess I'm scared to drive because I don't want to cause an accident. I don't know if that's a reasonable concern or if I'm just guilty of over-thinking again. For me to successfully run errands, I have to shut down my mind enough to drive without a ton of worry, and I have to make sure my body is ready for the trip so that I don't get symptomatic while I'm driving. It would be easy if I could predict when all this is going to happen. It's just kind of a confident feeling and I guess a leap of faith that my medicine will work enough to drive. When I get excited about driving somewhere successfully, it really is an accomplishment for me. Sometimes, I just don't think people understand how bad it can be, and also I don't want others to feel ashamed if they struggle with driving too.

16 WORKING AND THINKING

I LEFT MY LAST DOCTOR'S APPOINTMENT A FEW WEEKS AGO WITH A LOT OF THINGS to work on and think about. My two main challenges right now are driving/leaving the house and over-thinking. I've started to put together a Lego set, filling in crosswords, and trying to read, both for pleasure and education of my illnesses. I'm trying to improve my mood and patience with others. I always wonder how much I can actually control my reaction to things. I have an open relationship with my parents where I can say things like, "Give me a minute. It's time for my medication." and things of that nature. My weight has been a battle my whole life, so I'm always trying to improve my physical health, mainly through weight loss. I am doing a better job of that since the holidays have passed. I only weigh myself a few times a year, but I can tell by how my clothes fit. I would like to start walking in my neighborhood. Hopefully, I can get up the energy and motivation when it's warmer outside, but if it's cold and if it's time, I will walk in the cold. I am even smoking less and drinking less coffee. I have extreme OCD when it comes to my medication times, and I still refuse to take my medicine early, but I have relaxed and allowed to take them later than scheduled. It's a trick of mine to have more energy, but I would never skip a dose entirely, on purpose anyway. Journaling like this has always helped me cope, and I probably have enough material for another book, but I'm not planning on doing that. I might look for a writing job somewhere. "The medicine works" my doctor tells me, so I tell myself that when I don't feel great. It really is amazing how far I've come. I have a lot to work on, but I'm in a great position to do whatever I want to do with my life from here on out. I'm grateful and blessed in many ways.

17 SIGNATURE

I GOT A SMALL SHIPMENT OF MY OLDER TWO BOOKS TODAY. I WILL BE GETTING another shipment of my newest book on February 4, 2020. I always enjoy autographing them all. It's a personal touch, and I feel like a part of me goes with every copy. My super secret wish is that my signature would be worth money some day, and my friends could sell my books for a lot of money. I used to practice my signature in grade school because I dreamed of being a professional baseball player. I dreamed of signing baseballs and roaring fans in a packed stadium. I guess a writer is close enough haha. I just don't think I was meant to be rich because I don't love money enough. When I have money, the greatest joy I get is to share it. It's part of my desire to help others and make other people happy. There are downsides to having that kind of personality, but overall, it has worked out for me. I was able to drive my car again to give it some work with no real issues, and I had a nice dinner with my parents. I finished my Lego set I was working on, and I'm almost finished with my article for The Antioch Review that's due at the end of February. Just writing about some pleasant thoughts that I had this evening.

18 GENETIC PREDISPOSITION

I BELIEVE THAT MENTAL ILLNESS IS MOSTLY A GENETIC PREDISPOSITION THAT COMES to the surface after a variety of environmental factors take place. It would be hard to pinpoint exactly what led to my diagnosis(es), but most of it had nothing to do with anything I did wrong morally or otherwise. I guess what I am getting at is that it doesn't help myself or anyone else to beat myself up for past behavior or feel sorry for myself. I try not to fall into that trap. I have work to do, and I can't accomplish treatment goals or help others if I am constantly looking back and wondering what I could have done differently. The past is over. There's very literally nothing I can do about it now, so I have to ask myself 'Now what?'. My medication helps calm my symptoms, but I have to do a lot of the work myself to gain progress. I am testing my anxiety every day, more and more, and I have had some great results. What did I have to lose? A panic attack? I've survived hundreds of those. Whenever I try to leave the house, most of the time every signal in my body is telling me “No, you can't do that”. My brain is sending fear signals. I guess at some point I made a leap of faith that my medication will work and the fear would go away. If you are stuck in your progress, ask yourself what you have to lose. My memory isn't very good, but in the past year, I have made a lot of progress, and I have gained so much. If you have severe anxiety or other mental illness, please keep trying. It can get better. I can't promise you anything, but it has gotten better for me. I don't know how to give away that resiliency that comes with not giving up. All I can do is try to be a good example and tell you what has worked for me and that my life has gotten better. I never quit on anyone.

19 SOCIAL MEDIA ON MENTAL ILLNESS

Only a few people in my circle on social media talk about mental illness, and I only know them in a professional capacity. It helps me to talk about my illness because it helps others, which in turn, helps me. It makes me feel like my struggles are all worth it. So, I just want to mention that people "let themselves go" for a variety of reasons, but it tends to happen a lot with people with mental illness. Hygiene can be a big challenge, which includes things like taking a shower, weight control, and other personal cleanliness. I have lost over 50 pounds now, and of course I'm proud of myself, but I have a long way to go before I really feel like I'm at a healthy weight. I think it's important to celebrate small successes along the way, but I try not to get too comfortable. I'm not really ready to declare victory over my illness, and I probably never will. I am always on high alert for triggers and red flags, which may sidetrack my progress. I fail sometimes, but I always try to put forth the best effort I can. I took a shower this morning and did some personal grooming. I also went out to lunch with my mom. All of these things are victories over my illness in that I both couldn't do them before, and that these tasks are still hard for me. I guess what I am getting at is that I'm starting to feel better mentally/psychologically, so I hope it will be easier for me to lose weight and take better care of myself physically. Just trying to hang tough, live right, and do the right thing.

20 DOWNTOWN

I DROVE MYSELF DOWNTOWN AGAIN. I'M SO PROUD OF MYSELF AND JUST SO grateful and happy (not always). If some of you knew what I have bounced back from, you would be amazed. My recovery and recent success is really something special. The best gift that mental illness gave me was appreciating every little success along the way. This is a lifelong illness. There is no cure. I am going to have to manage it the rest of my life, but when I can enjoy life at the same time, the struggles don't seem so bad. I have made so much progress!

21 I AM AN AUTHOR

When I think of authors, I think about people like Stephen King and James Patterson, but not myself, for some reason. When I was a kid, authors of books that I read were just otherworldly or something. I never thought I would become one, especially three times over. I am lucky to know some amazing authors and writers, and they have taught me a lot. I always think that I couldn't be a writer for a living, but here I am, writing again. I've thought about getting my MA in Counseling or doing some public speaking too. This whole journey has been very surreal in a lot of ways.

When strangers meet me, a lot of the time, they say it seems like they have known me for years. I think I'm pretty transparent. What you see is what you get. Maybe it's good vibes or something. A lot of people confide in me, which is a compliment that people trust me so much with their life stories. I very rarely get overwhelmed with all of it. I just feel like this is what I am supposed to be doing right now. I haven't changed too much, and if I have, I would like to think I'm just a better version of my old self. I'm always trying to improve myself, and every day, I am getting better at coping with mental illness. I am surrounded by so many people that love me. It really helps me deal with life. It's also a pretty amazing feeling to think that I am helping others by simply telling my story, perhaps even saving lives. I've come so far.

22 POSITIVE IMPACT

I HOPE I HAVE MADE A POSITIVE IMPACT ON YOUR LIFE IN SOME CAPACITY. YOU probably don't have to read my books to know a lot of my story. If you aren't feeling well mentally, please reach out. There's the crisis line, or even calling the police or an ambulance. You can reach out to me, but I can only help so much if you need medical attention. I've lost a few friends to suicide and drug overdoses, and I want it to stop. 10-20% of bipolar sufferers die by suicide, and 50% have attempted suicide. One in five people has a mental illness. These are staggering numbers when considered to scale of the general population. I know I can't save everyone, but no one is going to stop me from trying. I guess I am a little greedy in that I want to have an impact on more than one person because a lot of people say, "If I could just help one person..." I want to help a lot of people, and I hope my story is read and told for many years after I expire.

23 MENTAL ILLNESS IS NOT FAIR

I'VE HAD 2 PANIC ATTACKS IN THE LAST TWO DAYS, AND SOME GENERAL ANXIETY. The panic attacks are less than a minute usually, but I was hyperventilating, which I haven't experienced in some time. General anxiety can last much longer. For me, it lasts until I eat a meal and take a nap. Mental illness is not fair, nor is life. I miss out on a lot of things to remain stable. If you think mental illness is "all in our heads", you are simply wrong and don't understand mental illness. I hope you never have to understand. It's physical, emotional, and psychological. It's a daily struggle to remain stable. I am physically sore and exhausted from the panic and anxiety. I had planned to go see my friends' band play today, but I simply don't feel up to it. I had been planning on it for months.

A panic attack that lasts a minute can bruise my ego and confidence. One minute is all it takes for me to be less confident about my progress. I am kind of a veteran of panic and anxiety, so I know I just have to build my confidence up again. I also know that a meal and a nap will take care of the problem. Just a little disappointed today, but I'm sure it will be better after I rest.

24 BOOKS

I don't know if this is a surprise to anyone, but I'm not that confident of a writer. Sometimes I think people are just being nice when they buy my books. Maybe they believe in supporting local artists. All of that is great, and I appreciate the support, but when you delve into my books, you will find more than a little valuable information about mental illness. My second book was a poetry book, which was more my creative side, but my first book is very clinical, and my third book is journal style, detailing life with mental illness. I say that my books have value because it's just an amazing story. Not a lot of people talk about mental illness, and a lot don't even survive for a variety of reasons. Then, for someone like me to have a clear enough mind to write about all of it. It's just a rare thing.

25 RAGE

I FEEL RAGE SOMETIMES. IT'S NOT RATIONAL ANGER. IT'S NOT ME, BUT I CAN GET fixated on something I don't like about life, or I can feel rage for seemingly no reason at all. Usually, it is when my medicine hasn't started working yet. I feel awful when I am mean to my parents, but they know it's not me acting out. They know it's not in my character. I always apologize if I think I was being irrational too. I have some things in place that I do that help ease my anger/rage until it passes. I want to share because maybe these techniques will help you:

I go into a quiet room. If I feel like listening to music, I put on relaxing music, emphasis on relaxing. Sometimes, I close my eyes and just breathe in and out in silence. I roll my own cigarettes, so that monotonous action helps calm me and helps spend unnecessary anger energy. I sit on my porch and have a cigarette, and watch the traffic go by. I try to think of myself as separate from the race everyone is running. I might text a friend and ask that person how their day went. I might crack jokes on social media to help cheer me up. I might go out of my way to be kind to someone else.

I am basically trying to distract myself and my rage long enough for the medicine to work. Rage is rare for me, but it's a strong emotion that I have. I absolutely hate it because it's not in my character or personality. I have a hard time being mean to people that deserve it, much less for no reason. Also, journaling like this helps too.

26 PLAYING WITH FIRE

For the longest time, I thought I was jealous of people who can drink alcohol all the time, have a good time, and still function. That's not it. Alcohol and drugs have and always will be there for me if I choose. Stability, productivity, sanity, and peace of mind were gone from my life for a long time, and I have been fighting very hard to get it all back. These are the qualities that I lost and that I value so much. I don't value being fucked up anymore. I don't need to self-medicate because my medicine works most of time. I have slip ups. I had 5 beers about a week ago, and I had a good time actually, but I'm playing with fire. Shit man, I'm playing with fire when I have something as harmless as coffee. Maybe I have more to lose now than I did before, because stability, sanity, and all those great qualities are priceless to me. I'm not willing to risk a night of drunkenness for everything I have fought for. Overall, I'm doing a pretty good job, all things considered.

27 PEP TALK

My really good buddy called me out of the blue around midnight a few nights ago. He just felt the urge to give me a pep talk of sorts, which I didn't think I needed at the time, but I did. He told me that I have to let the things go that I've done that I'm not exactly proud of. He's right. I think my biggest regret is not what I've done or not done, it's how much energy and guilt I gave to my regrets, and how much I cared what other people thought of me. All that really matters is who I am today, and I'm proud of that person. There's no need to beat myself for things that happened a long time ago. It's not fair to myself, and it's not productive if I want to help and love others. I think when we are young; we are taught to feel guilt and remorse for things we've done wrong, which is a good way to learn right from wrong, but at some point in our adult lives, we have to let it all go. I'm the only person I'm going to have to live with my whole life. I have to love and forgive myself, and I'm still learning.

28 GIFT OF MENTAL ILLNESS

I TELL PEOPLE ALL THE TIME THAT THE BEST GIFT MENTAL ILLNESS HAS GIVEN TO ME is an appreciation for the little things (which maybe are big things) and a general sense of gratitude. I was never a bad person. I just didn't fully appreciate how blessed I was, and I took life for granted. I use the word blessed instead of lucky or fortunate because I feel like blessed is a superlative word, and that's the degree to which I feel the gratitude, if that makes sense. When I use the word blessed, I am basically just describing the overwhelming sense of gratitude that I feel quite often now.

29 JUST BE YOU

My good buddy told me at my birthday party, "Just be you". Such a simple statement. This good friend thought that me being myself was good enough for him. I think we complicate things sometimes by always striving to be better and obtain more "stuff". There's nothing wrong with trying to better yourself and move up the money ladder, of course, but sometimes we define ourselves by status symbols and whatever else society says makes us good enough. Being myself is good enough for my friends, and that's actually an amazing thing, and takes a lot of pressure off me. I know how to be me. I can do that. I just want my friends to be themselves too. I wouldn't keep them around if I didn't think they were good, solid people. If you are a good person with good intentions, just be you. The world doesn't need more successful people (again, nothing wrong with that). The world needs more good, kind, and loving people.

I'm really proud of myself. I fought hard today. Today wasn't terrible, but it certainly wasn't easy. I had some anxiety and racing thoughts throughout the day, but I managed to do some housework, which helps calm me and also helps my mom. I shaved my face, which may seem very minor to most, but when I was first hospitalized in 2006, I had to earn the trust of the nurses to use a razor. Razors and sharp objects were only allowed by patients at the nurses' discretion for (hopefully) obvious reasons. I always think about the tiny drab community bathrooms and showers when I shave my face. Shaving my face is a reminder of the freedom I have earned in recovery, and it gives me a sense of pride every time I shave. I have traumatic memories from the hospital too, but shaving my face elicits mostly good feelings. I don't even take shaving my face for granted anymore. I am also budgeting money better this month and improving my general mood.

I use social media for a lot of the same reasons everyone else does—sharing memes and photos, random status updates, etc. I definitely like to make people laugh, but I also like to use social media for a purpose. I run my own page devoted to mental health awareness, and it's a great tool for a small time author like me to promote my books. Social media has also allowed me to stay in contact with so many people when I was super sick. I also like all the live music venue feeds because I can't always be there in person.

30 PILE OF BOOKS

I'M SITTING HERE LOOKING AT A PILE OF MY BOOKS THAT I ORDERED, AND IT'S JUST such a wild feeling that I turned out to be an author/writer. When I got a degree in psychology, I thought I was going to be a psychologist. Being a writer was something so far from my plans. You may as well told me I was going to be an astronaut. Weird how stuff works out sometimes when you think it isn't. I'm helping at least as many people as I would have had I become a psychologist. It's just such a weird feeling to look at a book and know that I wrote it. I'm not trying to toot my own horn or anything. Just being honest.

31 FIGHTING THIS ILLNESS

My anxiety got the best of me just now. I tried 3 times to get into my mom's car to go get my truck from having repairs, and I couldn't sit still, and I had chest pains from anxiety. The reason I had an anxiety attack or whatever it was, was because I had just taken my medicine and it hadn't kicked in yet (usually takes about an hour or so). Luckily, my awesome parents picked up my car for me, so now I don't have to worry about it. I can't stress enough how important it is to have support with mental illness. I am truly blessed with great friends and family who I know are always going to be there for me. Others are not as fortunate, which is one of the big reasons I try to be a good example by fighting this illness and trying to be there for others. Usually, the best cure for a panic attack like that is a good meal and a nap, so that's what I'm going to do.

32 NOT OKAY

IT REALLY FREAKED ME OUT WHEN I COULDN'T SIT STILL FROM PANIC AND RIDE IN MY mom's car yesterday. I had a doctor's appointment scheduled for tomorrow, and I had to reschedule. I contacted my case manager, and I told him I wasn't feeling well or confident enough to endure a doctor's appointment tomorrow. Props to my case manager for responding to my texts when he was out of the office. I told my parents I wasn't feeling well too. That's all I can do I think. I'm a little upset because I feel like some of my progress was taken away, but hopefully, I will be okay shortly. It's been a lot worse before.

33 STRUGGLES AND TRIUMPHS

The reason I write about my struggles and triumphs is to inspire others and make others feel like they are not alone. I'm not suffering. I struggle sometimes, and there's a big difference. I don't want anyone to feel sorry for me, but of course, I appreciate the support and prayers. I would rather you pray for people who are really suffering, but I guess there's enough to go around.

34 DR. PHIL

I'M NOT A BIG FAN OF DR. PHIL, BUT SOMETIMES MY DAD WATCHES HIS SHOW because it's on TV right before the local news. He was talking to a 28-year-old female drug addict today, and he said something very powerful. He said, "You are 28 years old. You might have another 60 years on this planet. If you get help now, this could all just be a bad memory." What a wonderful thought for anyone who wants to change or put their past behind them. Maybe parts of my life can just be bad memories too, and I can move on (if I haven't already).

35 INSPIRED

I'm going to sell however many books, but I really just want people to be inspired by my story. Maybe I can open some eyes as to what it's like to live with mental illness and how severe it can be, and how it's such a wide spectrum. Bills are bills, and money is money, but it doesn't matter to me if we have a chat about mental illness or you read about it in one of my books. It's just the same to me.

36 LIBRARY POEMS

My driving anxiety has come back in the last week or so, but today, I drove to the library to submit my second book, "Poems from a Bipolar Mind" for their catalog. This book should be on the shelves in the next month or so. No anxiety issues at all really. I was a little nervous when I left the house, but I'm really glad I was able to drive and get a little exercise. Anxiety and panic is only a little bit logical, so there's only so much that therapy can do. Usually, it's just a baby steps process to get back where I was, which I totally hate, but it is what it is. Just thankful I was able to overcome my fears today.

37 WHITE CASTLE

I just went to White Castle, and they were short 2 workers. They called off. Happens all the time in food service. Knowing this, instead of choosing to be angry and frustrated, I chose to just be happy that I was getting food that I was cheating on my diet. I was making conversation with other people in line, and smiling. I also gave the cashier a $5 bill and thanked her for showing up. We make lots of choices every day. Choose to be the bigger person and the exception to the rule. Maybe on another day, I would have been upset. I don't know. I just think today was the day to show compassion and humility to these human beings who were serving me food.

38 SHAKESPEARE

"THE ROBBED THAT SMILES STEALS SOMETHING FROM THE THIEF" IS A Shakespearean quote that I've always liked. I thought about going so far as to get it tattooed on me. I feel like when I have a positive attitude and sense of humor in the face of mental illness (The thief, if you will), I feel like I am getting something back that mental illness stole from me. Mental illness took everything I had at the time, and then it tried to take my life. I have survived over 13 years since those days many years ago. Looking back on my journey, a lot of people would call it a success story. I don't know about all that, but I'm definitely proud of how I have handled everything and how my life has turned out.

39 SINGING

I'M ALWAYS LOOKING FOR NATURAL WAYS TO ALLEVIATE MY BIPOLAR AND ANXIETY symptoms, and I read that singing out loud can help anxiety. This might explain why I don't have many problems singing karaoke, but why I still have problems driving to the bar to get there. Sometimes, I sing around the house without even thinking about it. Just a fun and weird thing about anxiety. I should say MY anxiety because what works for one person, might not work for another. That's why mental illness is so hard to treat, whether with cognitive therapy and/or medication. Everyone experiences mental illness differently.

40 DON'T WASTE YOUR LIFE

Sometimes, life can be overwhelming, and I let it get to me, and other times, I laugh at the magnitude of it all and my very small part in all of it. I laugh at all the dumb jokes I know or ironically, the daily tasks when they seem never-ending. Of all the atoms that could have formed anything, a tiny fraction made me and you. Yes, I know the science. The fertilized egg, yada yada yada. But there still had to be a pretty incredible happening to form your being. Don't waste it. Have something to offer to others. As far as I know and believe, we only get one shot at this thing, so make it memorable. I always keep love and kindness in my heart, which I think helps me deal with a lot of things. Oh yeah, and as much comedy as I can fit into a day without annoying others.

41 HEARTBREAK

I THINK BY THE TIME YOU GET TO BE MY AGE, YOU HAVE EXPERIENCED SOME KIND(S) of heartbreak and trauma that has left you a different person, if you are wise. I wish for myself that I have become a more grateful person, and a better all around person since I was first diagnosed. I lost everything—my house, my car, my mind, my reputation—literally everything. I have spent so much time trying to get my life back on track, with a lot of success. I never thought I would be an author and writer. I have touched many lives and helped many people, and that makes me happy and gives me purpose and the will to continue the journey. My mission in life has almost nothing to do with longevity, but rather making an impact. I'm not planning ongoing anywhere any time soon, but then again, no one really ever does. I want my life to be a celebration like the stupid birthday parties I have been throwing for about 10 years. I'm never going to be confident enough to say that I beat my illness, but it certainly didn't beat me.

42 EPISODIC

I will see the doctor in a few weeks. I'm starting to think about what I want to talk to him about, and it's frustrating. I feel like I should want to do things, but I'm not interested in a lot of things. My energy level is low, and I'm sore from being overweight and inactive for a few months. It looks like depression symptoms, but I'm not really sad. I had enough energy to write my third book, but I don't think it would take this long to recover. For a few months, I was going out and driving and really enjoying myself. When the time and weather changed, and I had a massive panic attack. It was like the rug got pulled out from under me again. It's so frustrating. I finally have enough money to do things and maybe take a trip somewhere, but I can barely drive up the street. Bipolar disorder is episodic, which is a hope I am holding onto right now, and that this is just another phase. I'm very grateful that I got out and drove places when I could. I always try to seize those moments when I feel well because lately I haven't been able to do much.

43 DEAR LAUREN

There was a courageous woman from my area who was diagnosed with a fatal brain injury. In her last days, all she wanted was letters of hope. Here is the letter I wrote her. She played basketball for a college called Mount St. Joseph's, and scored a basket in one of her final days.

Dear Lauren,

There is so much I want to say to you. I wish I could just talk to you over coffee or something. I also hope you get this message. You are such a hero to so many people, including myself. I hope you realize how big of an impact your story has had on everyone, near and far. You have shown everyone how to face adversity with dignity and courage. You have turned a negative into a positive. Even that is such an understatement. Your story will be told for such a long time. That is something so special. Your impact is on the same level as famous authors, scientists, and dignitaries. My friends and family are praying for you, and we all wish you a Merry Christmas! Keep fighting!

Love,

John Edward Medl, Age 33 Cincinnati

44 KINDHEARTED STRANGER

WEIRD HAPPENINGS ON THE PORCH THIS MORNING...A MAN STOPPED HIS CAR IN front of my house and started walking towards the porch. I thought it was my overdue package, but it was a guy my age who lived in the neighborhood. He said he drives by every day, and he saw me sleeping one day, and he wanted to make sure I was okay. He said it had been bothering him for a week because he didn't know if I was okay. I explained to him that I fall asleep sometimes on the porch because I'm groggy from medication. I told him I had bipolar disorder, and I take medication for it. He said he had bipolar disorder, too. He also has anxiety, panic attacks, and PTSD from the military. Same as me, although I was never in the military. He was 38 years old. I will be 38 in 9 days. He was first diagnosed in 2006. Same as me. This was just some random, kindhearted stranger from the neighborhood checking on me. So cool of him to do. Just a very nice, weird thing that happened this morning.

Having a positive attitude doesn't mean I'm happy all the time. I get in bad moods. Some (parts) of my days are bad sometimes. Mental illness and depression are very real and powerful, but if you start out deciding you are going to have a positive attitude, it's hard to say that you are a failure. I get enjoyment out of making people laugh and smile. I am also very candid about my struggles and illness. At the end of the day, when I'm laying in bed at night, I look back on the day. If I can look back on the day and see that someone was happier or inspired because of my life, I won that day. It's a daily measuring stick that I use to decide if I was successful for the day. I may not have had a great day, but if someone else did because of me, everything I go through is worth it. I am winning at life, despite everything. This is just simply my philosophy of life. It's not something that can be measured. It's not logical like mathematics. I'm just telling you what helps me get through hard days. I know it works because I feel it and live it.

I think most people know that bipolar disorder is a disease of extremes, especially moods. I am somewhat stable most of the time. I don't like it. I like being manic, but it's not good for me. I think I'm so addicted to coffee because it makes me manic sometimes, even at my anxiety's expense. Conversely, I can be in a good mood one minute, and the next minute, it feels like someone punched me in the gut with depression. It's strange and fascinating. I try my best to describe it.

45 DETACHED OBSERVER

Here's another poem and commentary I found from 20 years ago, when I was a senior at Moeller High School. Some of these old writings of mine are really weird because you can almost see and feel my mental problems coming on. This was written in the year 2000. I wasn't officially diagnosed until 2006. I guess it just feels weird to me because I wrote it and I remember vaguely how I felt. Like I said before, I'm still the same guy, and maybe my life turned out exactly how it was supposed to. I just took a few detours.

DETACHED OBSERVER

Don't want to ruin the mood,
I'd never think to intrude,
Upon such important matters dear to you.
I care about everyone else because of all I have felt,
I will emerge in the end,
To see the vision of mirth again.
Dissipate the groups I've come familiar with,
Take away the sanity, which fades to a myth.
Move me along the world with no trace of a journey,
For no trace for anyone to find myself.

Commentary

This poem I wrote when I started to feel that my life was becoming too hectic and rapid for my own mind. I felt that I would be lost in the shuffle of adulthood, and everything was going to change now that I'm entering the real world. I guess I'm scared, but more anxious. I wasn't a very happy person when I wrote this because I feel the pain of other people, and I'm oversensitive to negative occurrences in life. I think the world is coming down on me sometimes, and I wonder why I'm here. I think that I may have a mission on this Earth to just simply be funny and nice to others, and I think that's an important vocation. It seems rather simple, but I think I can help others a great deal in the field of psychology to help those who have struggled like myself.

46 GROWING APART

Do you think that others naturally grow apart as everyone gets older? I always wonder if it's because of my illness that I have lost so many friends and acquaintances. I don't want to believe that my former friends forgot about me on purpose or for any other reason than everyone is busy and has families now and such. When I go out, which is hardly ever, I'm trying really hard to keep the conversation about my books and my illness to a minimum. I care less about being liked, and more about being too much for people or having the conversation get too heavy when people just want to have fun. I also need a break. I have to deal with my illness almost every second, and then I'm advocating on top of that. I don't want my illness and work to define me. I have a lot of substance to my personality.

47 EMERGENCY WAITING

I remember sitting in the emergency waiting room. I was reading Bible verses to an older black woman. She didn't seem to mind. She was friendly. I remember that much. I went to use the bathroom, and my urine was bright orange, like orange soda. I'm pretty sure I was hallucinating. The doctors took me back into the treatment part of the building. I couldn't calm down. A doctor asked me a bunch of questions—if I knew who the president was and if I was on drugs. She asked me all the drugs I have done, and I had to answer with embarrassment in front of my parents. The nurses gave me a big shot of medicine in my right arm. Shortly after, I laid down in a bed in a room off to the side and slept peacefully for many hours.

48 POLITICS AND WAR

And everything was about politics and war
And now it's always more
Until everything had been bought from every store.
No one wants to leave home
Safety in their gadgets
All the information in the world,
And no one uses it.
Where do we go now?
What's it all for?
Nothing is much use if you don't
Venture from your doors.
To explore everything that has always been there
Just waiting to be enjoyed
But people would rather argue and play with their toys.

John E. Medl

I KNOW I'M A STRONG PERSON, BUT I GUESS I DOUBT HOW STRONG I AM GOING about this whole driving anxiety problem. There's a lot of moments in my life when I say to myself, "Wow. That took a lot of strength". You are a strong person. I guess I just wonder if I'm being too cautious about driving. When I have physical symptoms of anxiety and panic—chest pains, dizziness, numbness in limbs—I feel like I am a danger on the road. Not to mention these symptoms make it extremely difficult to drive.

49 I AM

I AM MANY THINGS. I'M A SON, BROTHER, AND UNCLE. I'M A ST. SAVIOUR GOLDEN Bear, a Moeller Crusader, and a Dayton Flyer. I'm a good person and a good friend. Some days I feel like I have the magic in me, and some days I feel like I'm just fighting to survive. One thing I am not is a quitter, and no one can take that away from me.

50 GRANDMOTHER

My maternal grandmother passed away around 1998-1999. Within days of her passing, I started to self medicate with drugs and alcohol. I never thought I'd be a party person like that. I think I was looking for emotional pain relief. I was hurt badly to a point that I had rarely experienced, if ever. In 2006, I was first hospitalized and diagnosed with bipolar disorder. She was a wonderful person. I've never met anyone so devoted to God. If there's anything after this life, I like to think she's looking down on us all, and that I've made her proud. We have a lamp that flickers from old wiring, and my mom says it's my grandma saying hello. It just happened, so I thought I'd write something about her. She never drove a car and loved getting her hair done. She liked a little wine, and she was a smoker, except for the last few years of her life. I guess it hurt so badly because I thought she'd always be there because she had always been there. I know this sounds like a sad post, but I'm actually reminiscing about her fondly before sleep.

A big problem I have is with confidence. In almost every sense of the word. With my mom breaking her wrist, I've had to do housework that she can't do. I don't know if I thought I couldn't take care of myself or what, but I'm learning that I can should I ever move out on my own. My mom has devoted most of her life to taking care of my dad and my siblings. With me doing some of the housework, it's a good reminder of how much my mom has done for all of us. I cooked dinner tonight for the most part. Laundry. Garbage. I don't take it for granted how much my mom does.

51 DISABILITY AND PUBLIC ASSISTANCE

I see stuff all the time on social media and wherever else that talk about people on disability or public assistance. It's almost always negative and judgemental. Yes, some people abuse the system and fake disability, but I don't believe that's usually the case. But guess what? It's not anyone's business. Yes, tax dollars pay for public assistance, but what about the people who become disabled who paid into Social Security for years? God forbid anything happens to you or your family where you need public assistance. Mr. or Mrs. Jones is allowed to have nice things even if they are food stamps. Maybe they bought their nice items before they became disabled. Maybe they have a rich uncle or something. You just never know. That's why being judgmental makes people look ignorant. Personally, it took me 7 years to get approved for disability. The whole process was ridiculous and nearly impossible. I had a lawyer, but I dumped every one finally, and I was losing hope. The way I got approved was my mother took all my records with a picture of me to the Social Security/Disability office, and shortly after, I was approved. It was a miracle for my family. I don't know where all these people are who are rich off the government, but it's not me. I would kill to be able to work a normal job. I would make a hell of a lot more money. My parents taught me the values of hard work, so I try to do what I can to feel like I am earning those disability payments and $38 a month in food assistance. I know not everyone is like that, but that's me. I don't worry about everyone else.

52 PANDEMIC

DURING THIS PANDEMIC, I SEE PEOPLE BEING KINDER TO EACH OTHER, IN GENERAL, of course. I see people respecting the elderly again. I see musicians finding new ways to perform. I see people making art and enjoying the outdoors. I see parents cherishing lost time with their kids. Maybe we needed a break and the world to stop for a minute... (obviously I know all of this has come at a great cost to a lot of people)

53 DEPRESSED

I'VE BEEN DEPRESSED FOR A FEW WEEKS OFF AND ON. IT'S ALWAYS OFF AND ON because of the duality of bipolar disorder. I've thought about what I might say if I knew it was the last of my time on Earth. I've thought about what my eulogy might sound like. Thoughts about death and dying are common with anxiety, depression, and bipolar disorder. There's as high as a 20% suicide rate for bipolar disorder as well. If I ever get to that point, I have faith that I would tell someone. Or write about it as I'm doing now. I've thought about my parents aging, and the real possibility that they might not be around some day. As always, the reason I'm writing this is for the greater good. You are not alone. If my symptoms aren't too bad, you can talk to me. Please get help if you need it or find an outlet that gives you relief.

54 NOTE FROM A READER

From a reader: Dear Mr. Medl,

I am a freshman student at the University of Vermont, enrolled in a class to discuss mental health disorders.

I have just read your book Millions Like Me, so I know reading is difficult for you.

Perhaps you have someone to help you read, but if not, I will try to keep this email short and space it so hopefully, it's easier.

I just wanted to say thank you for your book.

I do not currently think I have any mental disorders (I just turned 18) but this book was incredibly helpful and insightful for me, regardless.

I of course, cannot begin to imagine the work you put into writing it, but it's so valuable to learn from.

Your poems, while tinted with sadness and isolation, are truly powerful and beautiful to read.

Again, thank you.

55 ANOTHER REALITY

Going through psychosis and being delusional is a strange thing, especially when I snapped out of it and back to another reality. I remember a lot of the insane things I thought and acted upon, and it just hurts. I think because it's so embarrassing. Not to mention how painful it was to go through that trauma. People I've known for a very long time witnessed my insanity, and like I said, it's so embarrassing. I'm sure when some people think of me, they think of the insane things I did, and not the actual person who I really am. I am not my illness. I've had a lot of great times in my life, and it seems like good times are rare for me anymore. I get in moods where I get so agitated that not even my mother's voice is comforting. I think about how nice eternal silence is going to be. I don't really believe in complaining, but I still experience a lot of pain—physical, mental, and emotional. Some days, I think I'm ready to call it quits, or if my life ended, I would be fine with it. I've paid back society and done my time. This is what bipolar depression looks and sounds like. I'm lost as to what helps or what can help me bring me out of a funk like this. I can't even think straight except for negative and depressing thoughts. I hold on to the hopes that it will pass as it always does. It helps when I joke around and make people laugh, or when I feel like I really reached someone who is also struggling. I felt like I didn't really know what to do right now, so I wrote it down, and I feel a little better. I'm going to try to practice some self-care tonight and just take it easy. Find something relaxing to do. I haven't read a single page of any book in a while, and I have a lot of interesting books I want to read. Self care might mean taking a shower or watching something mindless on TV. I wish I could figure it out like a math problem, but depression is rarely logical.

56 MENTAL ILLNESS IS UNFORGIVING

I WAS SUPPOSED TO HAVE A PHONE CALL MEETING/ASSESSMENT WITH MY psychiatrist today, but he was out of the office. I was looking forward to it because I wanted to talk about some emotional issues I've been having lately. I got rescheduled for 10 days from now, so it's all good. As much as I've written, I don't think I've ever just flat out said that mental illness is really hard to deal with. Maybe a few times, but not often. I don't like talking about it, and I hate complaining and excuses. Mental illness and not having a properly functioning brain has BY FAR been the hardest thing I've ever had to deal with. The worst day of my life was when I was first hospitalized in 2006, although I wasn't completely coherent, but I remember more than I should. I've tried to make the most of my situation and stay positive by writing and cracking jokes, etc., but it's really hard on me sometimes. I know a lot of you out there have to deal with all sorts of things that maybe you don't talk about. No matter what the ailment, you are not alone. I struggle a lot too. Like I said, I do a pretty good job of playing it off, but my mental illness can be unforgiving.

57 MENTAL COMFORT

I HAD A MEETING OVER THE PHONE WITH MY PSYCHIATRIST TODAY. HE'S VERY positive. He reminded me of how far I have come and told me I am doing a good job. If I could only internalize what others see in me. I am an overthinker and my own biggest critic and enemy. Even after all this time, I am still a work in progress. I don't know if I will ever be satisfied. My doctor even said that he wishes he could put me on payroll to talk to some of his other clients. I have been completely compliant, especially with medication, which is not my nature at all. I put my trust in the experts' hands, and they delivered. Before my diagnosis, I never even took Advil or Tylenol, much less psychotropic medications. Somewhere deep down, I know I am a success story. I know I inspire people. I know I am blessed, and I am grateful for everything I have and everything I've worked for. I have a sick brain that tells me lies and sometimes I can't convince myself that I'm actually doing pretty well compared to my mental health history. I guess it was nice to hear from my doctor. I've been humbled to the point of rock bottom, but I still believe there is something special about me. I've emptied the tank, so to speak, for so long and so many days trying to fight this illness. It's exhausting and frustrating, but I've never quit, which is something to hang my hat on. When I try to sleep at night, I remind myself that I am doing the best I can to provide some sort of mental comfort.

58 LINGERING FEARS

I CONQUERED ONE OF MY BIGGEST AND LONGEST LINGERING FEARS TODAY. I SAW A primary care doctor and had blood drawn. It had been about 10 years since both events. Everyone who gave me medical attention was great. My blood pressure was a little high, but not concerning. The blood work is the standard tests—kidney and liver functions, sugars, and metabolism. I guess you can't just be fat anymore haha. I have faith and hope in humanity, even if it is only temporary. What matters to me more is having faith and confidence in myself. It's a lot easier for me to help humanity when I feel good about myself. I can't help anyone if I don't believe in my abilities. I don't need faith in humanity. I've seen what it is—good and evil, ups and downs, lies and truth. It's always going to be that way. I just try to do my part, and I can't do that to my fullest ability without confidence, faith, and trust in myself.

59 MANIA

There's noise coming from the magic box
As I roll up another cigarette
The actors have rehearsed their lines
Handed down to them by people
Who have never had to fight for anything
The brave warriors slave away
For a hundred dollars a day
If they're lucky
So the privileged can live in decadence
It's been this way for such a long time
When will this change like society has?
Fear and masks
All we know how to do is pray
I wonder if anyone is listening

Mania is a hallmark feature of bipolar disorder. When manic, a person can impulsively spend money or have trouble budgeting money. I have experienced this many times, and it's something I struggle with. Today, I was able to open my own checking account. For years, I have been sharing an account with my mom, and it has caused a lot of stress in my family. Glad to check another thing off the list, working towards more independence and responsibility.

60 HARDEST LESSONS

One of the hardest lessons I'm still trying to learn is that not everyone is going to like me. There's a saying that goes, "You could be the ripest, juiciest peach in the world, and there's still going to be people who don't like peaches". Honestly, it's their loss. I'm loyal to a fault, and I have a lot to offer. I would never screw anyone over intentionally, and I don't wish harm on anyone, not even the people who have done me wrong.

61 WHY NOT ME?

Sometimes, I think to myself, "Why does anyone care what I write about?", but then I think, "Why does anyone care what anyone writes about? Why not me?" I'm not some expert who is just writing about something I've read in books. I've lived the Hell that I write about. I think that's one of many reasons why people gravitate towards me and are interested in reading my books. If you read my books, you will find that I am brutally honest about my symptoms and my experiences. Just something to think about for any aspiring writers. I also hope that my honestly does not come off as complaining because sometimes I think there's nothing worse. It's a toxic trait that creates a negative environment. I try to be grateful and humble. It's a challenge. It's much harder to be grateful and courageous in the face of adversity than the alternative.

62 TREATMENT PLAN

Yesterday, I had a meeting with my clinical diagnostician, and today with my case manager. Relatively painless stuff. We basically laid out a treatment plan for the year. I wish I didn't have to do stuff like this, but it's probably for my own good. I really just want to be free and left alone most of the time, but all my meetings are good reminders of my goals and progress, I suppose.

63 RANTINGS

My parents are sleeping, so y'all are going to have to deal with my rantings. Before I wrote this, the office chair broke, which is supposed to have an 800 pound capacity or something. This is like the third one that has broken on me. I'm not slim, but I'm not 800 pounds.

We had to have a new sump pump installed in the basement today, which is basically not my territory of business, but it's just something that happened today.

The Department of Education forgave the remaining balance of my student loans years ago, but they still send mail to check up on me to make sure I haven't become wealthy or gainfully employed. Not a huge deal, but stressful and annoying in some small way.

Here's the really annoying thing. I started a checking account with $40 a few weeks ago, and it was overdrawn this morning. Every time I made a transaction, I checked the banking app first to make sure the money was there. When I set up the account, I told the people to make sure that no purchases would be approved if the money wasn't there. When I went to bed last night, I had about a dollar in my account, which is fine because when I set up the account, I made sure there was no minimum balance requirement. I MADE SURE all of these things to safeguard against an over withdrawal. When I woke up this morning, I had to deal with the stress of my account being way overdrawn, and not just by a little. No one at the bank wanted to take responsibility, and everyone around me just assumed it was my fault because I've had a few bouts of financial irresponsibility. I guess it's at least partially my fault because I was the one at the controls, but I was so careful. I was even keeping track with pen and paper because I felt like something wasn't right. Long story short, fuck today. Let's hope for a better tomorrow.

64 PANIC ATTACKS ARE NOT FOR THE WEAK

Panic attacks are shocking in a lot of ways. I'm not sure if that's the right word. I'm just always shocked at how painful they are and that I've survived so many. I just had a brief panic attack, and they are not for the weak. My entire body gets stiff, and my mind races in nonsensical words and phrases. I get dizzy and I get stomach cramps. I just took an Advil to try and kill some of the physical pain. Loud noises are almost unbearable to tolerate, but soft and familiar music sometimes helps me. I roll cigarettes to try and distract myself. I try to move around to make the body stiffness better. When my stomach settles, I'm going to eat dinner and rest. That's how I deal with them. It's over after that. Then the battle begins again. This doesn't happen to me often, and I've actually been making some good progress.

65 VICTORIES

Some victories that I've had lately:

1. I opened my own checking account so that I could be financially independent.
2. Some of my family members visited for dinner, so I got to see them. I had anxiety almost the whole time, but I got through it.
3. I successfully completed 3 meetings this week--- one with my clinical diagnostician, one with my case manager, and one with my psychiatrist. We laid out a treatment plan for the next year, and my medications are staying the same, but that may change. My doctor didn't want to change anything because he hasn't seen me in person for months. I've been on the same medication for about 8 years now.
4. I filled out some official paperwork regarding the forgiveness of my student loans
5. I drove myself to the store and to the bank. I have major driving anxiety, and sometimes I can't drive at all.

All of these things are hard for me. They are challenges and considered victories when I complete them. I think I had too many things going on in one week, so that's probably why I have had increased anxiety and panic attacks.

66 ARE YOU HEARING VOICES?

WHENEVER I HAVE A VISIT WITH MY PSYCHIATRIST, HE ALWAYS ASKS THE SAME beginning questions...."Do you think you can fly or do you think you have superpowers?" and "Are you hearing voices?". These may seem like strange questions to the average person, but I have answered "yes" to these questions before. Quick example. When I was first hospitalized in 2006, I was convinced that I could jump off the balcony at the hospital and "fly" or land safely below. I have no idea what stopped me. I have a "loud brain", which basically means I have an active inner dialogue. Not everyone has that, so I've found out. It serves me well with writing, but it's extremely annoying and exhausting when I'm trying to rest. As long as the "voices" aren't directive (telling me to do a specific thing), then I'm considered stable enough, I guess. I've had problems with directive voices/psychosis before also. I can only explain psychosis as watching myself in a movie and someone or something else is at the controls. I've always had a loud brain, but I haven't had problems with psychosis or extreme grandeur in a long time.

Am I angry at life because of my mental illness? Not usually. I don't see how that's productive, and the world doesn't owe me anything. It could always be worse. Even when I don't have any money, I'm richer than a lot of people across the world. I wish I were a stronger person so that I acted as blessed as I feel, but I'm just human with limitations. I've tried not to use my illness as a crutch, but it is a good explanation for a lot of my behavior. For me, mental illness is frustrating, painful, and exhausting. I've prayed for death and thought about taking my own life. My best days are when I get some relief. It doesn't happen often, as my illness is mostly relentless. I've chosen to educate others through my books and volunteer my time to help others find some relief. So many positive things have come from my illness, and it helps me to focus on all the good things rather than feel sorry for myself.

67 RACIAL PROTESTS

June 9, 2020: In the middle of a global pandemic and racial protests

I don't feel guilty for being white. I didn't get to choose my skin color as much as anyone. But I do understand what white privilege means. As a white person, I'm more likely to have access to all kinds of resources and less likely to be harassed by the police. It doesn't mean that my life is easy. I know good cops. I've known them almost my whole life. But once you are mistreated by the police, how do you forget that? My former professor is Latino and he was brutalized and beaten by police in Minnesota. He won a lawsuit against them. I'm seeing a lot of positive changes in the form of diversity programs and funding for minority causes. It's very strange as a white person. I think I was so used to everyday racism that I was comfortable. Change is usually uncomfortable, and I want to be part of the solution, and I want to be on the right side of history. If racial equality is going to happen, white people need to help because we're still running the show.

I had a pretty good day today:

1. I took a shower. Embarrassingly, it had been a while.
2. I balanced my checking account, and the balance is positive.

3. I drove myself to the doctor for a sore jaw. He prescribed me antibiotics for the infection. I'll probably have to see a dentist, barring some miracle, but still a victory for me.

I've got to learn to not be so hard on myself

68 BLESSED

I'M A LUCKY, BLESSED MAN. EVERYONE IS SO KIND TO ME, ESPECIALLY MY MOM, THE rest of my family, and close friends. I know this sounds stupid, but I feel like if I remind myself of my blessings even in hard times, that I will somehow heal faster. In a way, it does help me heal faster. Reminding myself of my good fortune at the very least occupies my mind with positive thoughts. I'm a simple man. I don't need much to be happy.

69 MANIA HIGH

MANIA IS OFTEN REFERRED TO AS A "HIGH", LIKE A DRUG. IT'S LIKE THE HIGHEST you've ever been off drugs that are in your brain. No street drugs compare. That's how intense it is. I've heard, "Medication took my superpowers away." That high. Delusional and psychotic high.

70 NOTCH IN MY BELT

I'VE HAD PROBABLY THOUSANDS OF PANIC ATTACKS, BUT I REMEMBER THIS ONE IN particular. I remember smoking 9 cigarettes in a row. I just couldn't calm down. It goes that way sometimes. I remember because I counted. It's an OCD thing. I also roll my cigarettes in even numbers because I smoke 2 in a row while I'm out on the porch. I will always contend that mental illness is the hardest thing I've ever had to endure. Every day I survive is a notch in my belt. I'm extremely proud of myself for never giving up.

71 DELUSION

I SHOULD HAVE KNOWN SOMETHING WAS WRONG IN COLLEGE, BUT THEN AGAIN, I showed symptoms in high school and childhood. We all just had no idea. In college, I engaged in risky behavior, but I had this delusion that lights turned off when I was around. Like street lamps. It seemed like it had happened a lot. Then, I told my friends, and they noticed too, which reinforced my delusion. The logical explanation is that these lights were on timers, and it was coincidental that the lights would turn off. I thought it was some kind of supernatural thing, but I didn't take it very seriously and kind of brushed it off.

72 LIFE ISN'T A WALK IN THE PARK

One of my best friends visited the other day. He's known me since high school. He visited me in the hospital and has bought all my books. I try not to talk about my illness in regular conversation, but it always seems to come up. It occurred to me that I never really asked about this friend's mental health. So I simply asked, "Do you have depression or anxiety or anything?" And he simply said, "No". It kind of blew my mind because I thought about how nice it would be to not have anxiety or depression, but I do remember a long time ago when I didn't have to worry about my mental health. It's an incredible blessing to not have to deal with. However, my buddy has physical health problems that I don't have to deal with, so his life is far from being a walk in the park.

73 14 YEAR SURVIVOR

On July 31, 2020, I will celebrate being a 14 year survivor of mental illness from the first time I was hospitalized. Mental illness tried to take my life many times, but my spirit was not having any of it. I really hope I get a chance to talk to the students of Moeller HS about mental health. When I attended Moeller, there wasn't much talk about mental health. All the advocacy work I do makes me feel like I'm fulfilling my purpose. That somehow, some way, makes me feel I am exactly where I am supposed to be, and I'm doing exactly what I am supposed to be doing. It's a great feeling to feel like you are fulfilling your purpose in life. The fear of dying with unfinished business goes away. The age old question of "Have I done enough with my life?" goes away. Whatever I have sacrificed for stability (most of the time), I have gained in perspective and purpose. I am extremely grateful for my life and how it turned out. I wasn't always so optimistic. I had to work at it. I've lost plenty of battles, but I feel like I am winning the war. That's as close to beating mental illness as you can get, in my opinion.

I just want to talk about intelligence for a minute because it's on my mind. I am going to describe my family because there are 7 of us (my parents and 5 siblings) because I think it is a good example of the varieties of intelligence. You don't need a college degree to be smart, but I think it helps. I also know people who didn't graduate high school who are master musicians and carpenters.

I guess I will start with my dad. My dad has a two-year degree from The University of Cincinnati. He is an electrical engineer by trade. He must be good with money too because we don't have a whole lot of it, but we rarely go without necessities. My mom didn't finish college. It wasn't really a popular thing for women to do in the 1960s. However, she has raised 5 kids with good values and morals with not too many injuries haha. She is an extremely hard worker, which I think is a type of intelligence in a way. She is also very organized, which I think is another kind of intelligence. My oldest brother is a radar specialist for a government contractor out in Arizona. He has a Master's Degree. My next brother never finished college, but he is a master carpenter and very good with investing and money. My sister never finished college, but she is an office manager who oversees collecting invoices for a billboard company. My closest brother has a Master's Degree in Mathematics and is extremely book smart and computer smart. He's the brother we call when our computer screws up. Then there's me, the youngest of all of us. I consider myself intelligent, but like everyone else, I have my moments of dim bulbness. I just wanted to write about my family because I love them all, of course, but I think we are all intelligent in our own way. Some of us have degrees, and some don't. It doesn't have to be an either/or thing where you are smart if you have a degree, and dumb if you do not. All of this probably just relates to the fact that you shouldn't judge people, and it seems like it comes down to that a lot.

74 OUT OF CONTROL

My spending was out of control this month, so I gave control of my finances to my brother. My checking account is closed, credit cards are frozen, and I don't have any way to move money with apps like Venmo and PayPal. I'm a little disappointed in myself, but I know it's for the best. I was borrowing money from a lot of people, mainly to gamble, and it had to stop to get this household's finances in order, and also to plan for the future. Gambling gave me hope that I could win a lot of money in a short time because I can't work in a standard job. The writing job I was hoping for isn't going to work out either. On the bright side, I drove myself to the store, and I'm getting closer to finishing my fourth book each day. I'm just having a difficult time.

75 HEAVENLY

So here's a story that I've never told before. Damn, I remember it like it was yesterday. It was at least 10 years ago at Good Samaritan Hospital. I was being treated for psychosis and panic. One of the nurses gave me a pill and asked me how I felt.

"Heavenly," I said.

I was looking out into the sun-setting sky, and that's really how I felt. Several times. I've felt a supernatural force acting upon me, usually good, but sometimes evil feeling. I found out later that the pill was just for heartburn, but I think I answered in that way because that's what I thought the nurses wanted me to say. I'm not really sure. I do vaguely remember actually feeling that supernatural, heavenly way. I don't think anyone can truly understand psychosis and mania unless you have been through it. I don't care how many degrees you have. You have to feel it and experience it. Some people describe mania as a high, but that doesn't fully encompass the feeling. It's not like a let's smoke a blunt in high school high. It's like the best drug you have ever taken, combined with the worst hallucinogenic drug you have ever taken times a million. And psychosis is like watching yourself in a movie, with someone else at the controls.

76 NOT TAUGHT TO QUIT

When I was 618 pounds, I should have just hung it up and let nature take its course. I didn't. I don't use a scale, but I'm almost certain that I've lost over 100 pounds. Every time I was hospitalized, people would have understood if I quit. When I had to take medication, that made me feel absolutely awful. I should have given up. When I was lying on the couch in a medicinal haze, I should have just stayed down. I kept getting up and forcing myself to take showers when it felt impossible. When I had panic attacks while driving, people would have understood if I quit trying to drive. I wasn't raised that way. We (my siblings) weren't taught to quit. We were taught to fight. Our parents led by example in many ways, but the most impressive was that my mom and dad each beat cancer twice. My dad only has one kidney. In all honesty, I don't know how I survived a lot of things I have. I don't know why I didn't quit when I didn't know what I was doing. My mind was gone, and I still didn't quit. Now, I'm about to be an author for the fourth time. I'm going to be mentioned in the Fall Newsletter for my alma mater, Moeller High School. I'm also trying to get a mention from my college alma mater, The University of Dayton, but they have been unresponsive to my messages. I've worked with the Cincinnati-based non-profit 1N5.org on several projects. I'm the founder and administrator of a social media page devoted to mental illness and inspiration for 8 years now. We have almost 800 members. At times, I don't know how I've come this far, but I'm glad I did. Yes, I'm bragging about myself. I've earned it.

77 SURVIVED ANOTHER YEAR

WELL, TODAY'S THE DAY. I SURVIVED ANOTHER YEAR. FOURTEEN YEARS AGO TODAY (July 31, 2006), my life fell apart. I lost my house, car, job, girlfriend, and any reputation I had as a sane person. I was rushed to the hospital with what they call a psychotic first break of bipolar disorder. I stayed in a locked down psychiatric unit for 11 days. It was a nightmare, and I still have flashbacks sometimes, even after all these years. I am extremely proud of how I have handled all my diagnoses and what I have accomplished. I have made my family and friends proud. I have a grateful and loving heart. I appreciate life now more than I ever did before. I tell everyone that I am blessed. I have everything I need, which is more than a lot of people have. At some point in my recovery, I decided I wanted to do more than just survive and exist. I've made lemonade, as they say, and I've played the cards I have been dealt to the best of my abilities. I can't express enough my gratitude for all the support, in every capacity. The love that has been shown to me, by all sorts of people, has been tremendous. I am just a humble servant trying to carry out a mission of kindness and awareness of mental health issues. Thank you all support for being there for me. It absolutely makes a difference.

78 BACK IN TIME

I DON'T WANT TO BE YOUNG AGAIN, BUT IF I COULD GO BACK IN TIME FOR A weekend in high school, I think I would agree to that. Party all weekend without a care or responsibility. Barely sleep, except on Sunday to recover for the upcoming week of classes. No smart phones or every app imaginable. Not many people had cell phones, either. I can't remember if I did or not. I remember people having pagers, which I never had. No Netflix and the like or social media. We took pictures with disposable cameras and actually had to wait to get the pictures developed. Weekend long binges at music festivals with a bunch of mostly kindhearted strangers just camping and listening to music. I think of those days fondly, but I still would only want to go back for a weekend. I enjoy my life now as a writer and mental health advocate. I appreciate peace of mind and silence. I don't like party atmospheres anymore. I don't think I'm boring. I just lived the party lifestyle already, and I'm done with it all. I want to keep those fond memories just as memories, and thank my lucky stars that I survived. Now, at age 38, I feel like I don't know about so many things, and I was so confident, borderline cocky in high school, which is amazing, because I was incredibly stupid compared to now. But I would still go back for a weekend if I had the chance. Maybe I am just feeling nostalgic today.

79 NOTHING IS BLACK AND WHITE

I USED TO BELIEVE IN THE GOOD IN EVERYONE. THE WORLD HAS SHOWN ME THAT'S not true. I used to think that bad people were just good people who did bad and evil things. I think people either chose to be evil or they are born that way, or some combination. That's usually how it goes in psychology. Nothing is really ever black and white. On a psychology exam, the answer is rarely straightforward. The answer is usually all of the above, none of the above, or both A and C. Things like that. I studied out of a philosophy book that was titled, "Taking Sides", and if I remember correctly, it was all about how people don't have to always take a side on every topic. You can agree or disagree with some parts of one side or the other. I think people get trapped into thinking in black and white terms, so when they are confronted with conflicting evidence of their beliefs, they won't give an inch because they have chosen a side. It's very hard for people to change their minds once they are made up. I believe this is the spirit of cognitive dissonance.

I remember writing a whole term paper on rationalization. It was either a psychology or philosophy course. In many ways, those two subjects overlap and are related. Anyway, the thesis of my paper is that rationalization is extremely dangerous because you can rationalize almost anything. Right now, I am fighting a gambling addiction. I have been gambling half of my life. It turned from recreational to a maniacal addiction. I don't like to use bipolar disorder as an excuse, but it definitely is an explanation and played a role. I was so stressed out about my parents' finances and their health. Every time I gambled, I thought I was going to win. It's really hard to give up because I have won a lot of money gambling. It was getting to the point where I was borrowing money and losing control. It had to stop. Maybe one day, I can recreationally gamble again, but for now, I am sickened by the idea, and I am trying to find myself again and finish this book. Getting back to my point, I rationalized my gambling habit because I don't drink alcohol or do drugs. I thought my gambling was acceptable because I didn't have those other coping mechanisms that most people have. You can rationalize anything if you lie to yourself enough.

80 COPING

I don't even know where to start. Last night, I was extremely depressed. I was watching a poker tournament on my phone, and I was just thinking about how nice it would be to have the money to play. I've been in a poker club for about 10 years now, and the tournament entrants were my friends. We usually play in person, but because of the pandemic virus, everyone plays on an online computer application. I haven't been able to play in person for several years now, with the exception of one night, because it's hard for me to concentrate that long and sit still. The key to live poker is to be as unreadable (a la poker faced) as possible, and my anxiety gives me away every time. It's not even fun anymore.

My checking account is closed. All my credit cards are cut up and my credit is frozen. I have no access to any gambling sites on the computer. I have no access to money applications on my phone to move money around. All of this is for the betterment of myself and my situation, as well as lightening the worry and burden on my parents and siblings. I know that. I'm trying to accept that. I don't know if I need a night out with my friends or if I need someone to visit me, or what. Sometimes I just feel like running away and starting a new life. I think about living in a tiny place with few possessions by a body of water and just living there until I die without talking to anyone again. I feel stuck. I don't know if I should live here with my parents or go start a new life somewhere. I don't even know if I could handle living on my own or afford it, for that matter. I don't want to abandon everyone, but I really do get that urge a lot. Maybe I'm just tired or anxious or otherwise symptomatic right now. I could barely sit still enough to write this entry.

Journaling is a coping mechanism for me, but it's also a force where I feel compelled to write like my brain needs to throw up, per se. Writing helps release the pressure in my mind of all my thoughts. I wonder if other writers or artists or musicians feel that creative force too.

I don't know if it's possible for the living to understand suicide, but I feel like I do. A long time ago, I was suicidal, but I never attempted it. I've had suicidal thoughts too. Mental illness and anguish is incredible pain, and my best guess is that it gets to be too great for some people. I don't think people who commit or attempt suicide are cowards. I think they're just humans who have had too much pain to bear. My writing and mental health advocacy have given me purpose, which helps me when my thoughts get dark. I don't really have suicidal thoughts anymore. I've had to call my case manager several times because I was in mental anguish, and I'm always confident that I will ask for help if I need it. I know the world is a better place with me in it. I know my family and friends would be sad, and I want to go down swinging with dignity. Even with all these great reasons to live, the dark thoughts still creep in sometimes. Mental illness is incredible pain, as I mentioned. Most of the time, I feel okay. I feel good about my life and my contribution to society. But the small amount of time when I am symptomatic is incredibly painful.

It is currently August of the year 2020. I live in Cincinnati, Ohio. There's a global pandemic ravaging through the world with staggering infection rates and fatalities. I don't know if life will ever be the same again. I'm hoping and praying that the pandemic eventually subsides, and a sense of normalcy returns.

81 NAMI

I will have 7 more copies of my newest book around September 24, 2019. Around that time, I will be shipping a variety of my books to NAMI (National Alliance for Mental Illness) in New Mexico, totaling around 10 copies. Thanks to my readers, friends, family, and even strangers who love and support me. It truly makes a difference. If I hear that I'm doing the right thing from others, it seems like life has been treating me well, which I take as a sign from the universe that I am doing the right thing. I am wise and humble enough to not declare victory just yet over my illness. It's going to be a lifelong battle. I hope I am up to the challenge. So far, so good I guess. Whatever mental illness has taken from me, I have gotten back exponentially, and I am grateful and blessed.

82 SUPPORT TEAM

Every so often, I like to thank my whole support team, which includes my readers, family, and friends. It makes a world of difference in my fight to stay positive and stable with my illness. Kindness matters. A few months ago, a woman at the grocery deli called me fat to someone she was talking to on her phone. I still think about it. It hurt a little bit emotionally, but I know I am doing the best I can to control my weight, and I also know I have been big my whole life. My point is that this woman probably had no idea the physical, emotional, and mental strength it took me to drive myself to the grocery. This was a time when driving for me was near impossible, and social interactions made me extremely anxious. She also didn't know that I had $5 to my name, and all I wanted was my favorite pasta salad to treat myself. Would she have cared had she known all of that? Maybe, but probably not. The world has gotten more unkind over the years, in my opinion. A lot of people have a psychological need to put others down to make themselves feel better about their own lives, which they are probably unsatisfied with, hence this psychological need to put others down. "In a world where you can be anything, be kind". Simple words from Dr. Seuss, but it can make a huge difference. I am lucky and blessed to have so many who support me and my writing. I care more about others being comforted by my story than any amount of money I make off my books. I donate them whenever I can. If you think my story is disturbing or outstanding or tragic or whatever, you should see some of the cases of people who have no support. So, a simple thank you to all of you. I would like to take credit individually for my successes, but I am not much of a success without all of your support. I think of myself as a humble servant or vessel just carrying out a mission.

83 ATTITUDE

My attitude has been pretty shitty off and on lately, and that's on me. It's a little more challenging to control my emotional reaction to things because of my illness, but I'm not the guy who likes excuses. I drove to the tobacco store today, which is only a few miles away, but I didn't have much anxiety. I was worried that I was relapsing or something, which would have been devastating to my confidence. I can't tell you how annoying it is for me to have to wait almost an hour to be calm enough to drive, BUT I'm thankful I have a car and that I can drive at all because I used to pretty much be confined to the house. With me, it's all about perspective and gratitude, and I lose sight of everything I'm blessed with sometimes. I'm a good person, and I know it, but I'm not perfect, and I know that too. No one is.

84 CHANGED

LESSON,MY ILLNESS HAS CHANGED ME IN MANY WAYS, SOME FOR THE BETTER, AND some for the worse. I would like to think more for the better. I have trouble relating to a lot of people because they just don't have an illness to contend with on a daily basis, so their priorities and outlook are different than mine. I really just want to make a difference through my books and otherwise, and be happy most of the time. Anything above that is great too. I've had more money than I could spend, and I was definitely happy. I bought a bunch of stuff I didn't need and went to bars and bought everyone drinks. I had a great time, but I didn't save a dime. I learned my lesson I guess. I still have trouble budgeting money, but it's not like I have some kind of million dollar trust fund to work with. I know that the white picket fence idea is not for me, at least not for the time being. I guess I understand the draw to that kind of life, but I'm selfish with my time and energy, and I'm not willing to share it with anyone right now in a relationship kind of way. I have plenty of people who love me in a familial and friendly way to keep me busy with my love. I guess it's hard to explain, and I certainly don't owe anyone an explanation, but everything changed when I got sick.

85 MENTAL ILLNESS ISN'T POPULAR

My books and my writings about mental illness will never be popular or well circulated. There are many reasons for that. Most people simply don't care about mental illness at all. The ones who do care either have an illness or someone close to them has it. Even some people with loved ones who have mental illness don't care. Some people don't even believe in modern medicine to treat mental illness. But, oh don't people love to blame mental illness, especially mass shootings, since they somehow have become trendy and popular. Everyone is in denial that the US has a gun problem. People actually think that people like me want to take their guns. Most people, even in their right mind, aren't responsible enough to own guns. They are dangerous killing weapons. Some guns' sole purpose is to kill as many people in as short a time as possible. Oh, but it's the mentally ill that's the problem. It couldn't be the access to guns. Then you have people who suffer from mental illness who are ashamed to even talk about it. Gee, I wonder why. The mentally ill are demonized by most of society and pill shamed if they need to take medicine.

86 PAPERWORK

I HAVE A MEETING WITH MY CASE MANAGER TODAY. HE HELPS ME A LITTLE BIT WITH cognitive therapy, but mainly, he helps me fill out all the long, confusing paperwork associated with my illness. He was a Green Beret, which I think is cool, so I will have to wish him a belated Happy Veterans' Day. He was shot in the back in combat, and he's had back problems ever since. I think he fought around the time of the Vietnam War. I don't have to see the doctor until January 6th, so another "fun" thing I have to do is get my medication refills approved so that I have enough medication until I see the doctor. You have no idea how many times I've wanted to say to my doctor, "Okay, I'm ready for the good shit" haha.

87 MURKY INDIFFERENCE

My medicine is designed to keep my mood and behavior somewhere in the middle of the mood and behavioral spectrum, and it does for the most part, but it results in this murky indifference and numbness. If I ever feel emotions like sadness or happiness, they are usually to the extreme, and usually accompanied by anxiety. I absolutely hate being in a bad mood, and I try to do things that make me happy to get out of that mindset. I enjoy lots of things—reading, music, watching sports, talking with friends, acts of kindness, etc. etc. etc. Most of the time, these things help my bad mood, but I have a feeling I don't experience emotions like most people. There's no concrete way to know, but I know a lot of people, and they don't seem to have the same emotional spectrum as I do. Just something interesting I've observed about my illness.

88 FED UP

EVEN THE BEST OF US GET FED UP—I'M SICK OF ALL THE PAPERWORK THAT GOES along with being on government assistance. I'm sick of doctor's appointments and medications. I'm sick of being sober because I'm so worried about everyone else's health, and if something happened when I was drinking, I would feel completely awful. I would lose so much progress, but again, I'm worried how my actions affect others. I think that a night out with my friends would solve these frustrations, or maybe even just a nice meal and nap, but don't think that I don't get upset and angry about all of this. I've been compliant ever since I entered treatment, but it's not my nature at all. I just hope I can settle down enough to continue to be on every else's time and schedules. I try my best to not complain and be a good boy and comply, but trust me, I want to break free of everything sometimes.

89 SURVIVAL MODE

Many years ago, when I was in an emergency situation, my instincts and survival mode kicked in. And some sort of amazing pain tolerance that I have no idea where that came from. I don't really see surviving the emergencies I've had as courageous. What took courage was facing the aftermath each time, and dealing with mental illness day after day, week after week, year after year. I may have given up if I didn't have some solid support from family, friends, and readers of my books. I mention this because a few people have stopped by lately just to see me, and one of my friends brought me some homemade food. I just want people to know that kindness and support like this matter to people with mental illness, and I would think anyone, really. So many people don't have this kind of support, and that makes a negative difference, too. I don't really know what my point is here. I guess I just want to say that the support I have has helped me greatly, and if you are able, be that support for others. It matters.

90 STRIPPER

HERE'S MY FUNNY STORY FOR THE DAY TO MAKE YOU LAUGH. MY MOM WILL probably kill me, but oh well, I'll just unfriend her on social media again haha. So....I've only been to the strip club as a patron a few times. Not really my thing. But when I was working as a pizza delivery driver in Dayton, Ohio, we delivered to 3 strip clubs in our area. One night, I got such a delivery to a place called Pizazz (lol). Not classy at all. As soon as I walked through the door, I was in the middle of everything. I bring a pizza over to these 3 businessmen type people, and they tell me to sit down and have a drink with them. First of all, I wasn't old enough to drink, and second, I was driving all night. When I turned down the drinks, they gave me a $10 tip and told me to sit down and called over a stripper. They explained to me that I was going to get a lap dance too, whether I liked it or not. They didn't have to twist my arm or anything, but I felt so awkward because I'm pretty shy about this kind of thing. To make it even more awkward, when the stripper is doing her thing, she says, "MMM, you smell like pizza" WTF? I have no idea what I'm supposed to say. 'Oh yeah baby, it's a meat lovers'. I can get you pizza all night long. LOL. Anyway, hope that made you laugh. True story, of course.

91 ETERNAL DIRT NAP

There's nothing for me on the other side
And I'm fine with that
Even if it is just an eternal dirt nap
What if there's more?
I'm tired and sore
I'm tired of thinking
My thoughts have always been my enemy
I just want to live silently
Head down.
Put in my days.
I just want to feel the sun's rays.
But the rain has its place.
You might even see a smile on my face
I want to feel content enough to be kind
My mind has failed me
But I trust my heart
Even when I fell apart

92 EULOGY

I'VE BEEN DEPRESSED FOR A FEW WEEKS OFF AND ON. IT'S ALWAYS OFF AND ON because of the duality of bipolar disorder. I've thought about what I might say if I knew it was the last of my time on Earth. I've thought about what my eulogy might sound like. Thoughts about death and dying are common with anxiety, depression, and bipolar disorder. There's as high as a 20% suicide rate for bipolar disorder as well. If I ever get to that point, I have faith that I would tell someone. Or write about it as I'm doing now. I've thought about my parents aging, and the real possibility that they might not be around some day. As always, the reason I'm writing this is for the greater good. You are not alone. If my symptoms aren't too bad, you can talk to me. Please get help if you need it or find an outlet that gives you relief.

AFTERWORD

This book is random in a lot of ways, but I wanted it to be that way. Mental illness can be very fluid and different every day. I think the goal of any treatment and medication regimen is stability, but it doesn't always work that way. I can have a span of a month where every day is a different battle, but I can also have a span of a month or several that are stable and much easier to contend with. I can't tell you exactly when I wrote all of the entries in this book, but I think it represents the volatility of my illness and mental illness in general. When I decided to become a writer and mental health advocate, my main goal was to bring awareness to mental health issues and to make others feel like they are not alone. I hope I have done that in this book and all my books. Much love to you all.

ALSO BY JOHN MEDL

Millions Like Me: My Struggle with Mental Illness: books2read.com/Millions-Like-Me

Poems From a Bipolar Mind: books2read.com/Poems-Bipolar

The Last Day of July: 13 Years of Madness: books2read.com/Last-Day-July

The Entropy of Bipolar Disorder: books2read.com/Entropy-Bipolar

Mental Illness Is An Actual Illness: books2read.com/Mental-Illness-Actual-Illness

Making Bipolar Lemonade: books2read.com/Bipolar-Lemonade

Bipolar Rising : books2read.com/Bipolar-Rising

ABOUT JOHN MEDL

John Medl is an author with over five published books and a mental health advocate from Cincinnati, Ohio. He has suffered from mental illness for more than eleven years. His diagnoses are: bipolar disorder with psychotic features, obsessive-compulsive disorder, Post-Traumatic Stress Disorder, Generalized Anxiety-Panic Disorder, claustrophobia, and agoraphobia.

John has a Bachelor of Arts in Psychology from the University of Dayton, which he finds ironic.

books2read.com/John-Medl

facebook.com/john.medl

twitter.com/johnmedl7

instagram.com/johnmedl7

amazon.com/author/john-medl

www.ingramcontent.com/pod-product-compliance
Lightning Source LLC
LaVergne TN
LVHW052038200926
848481LV00005B/1718
* 9 7 9 8 2 1 5 0 3 0 7 7 6 *